GARDEN

TO GUT

COOKING YOUR WAY TO VITALITY
THROUGH LONGEVITY

DORINE MWESIGWA

FOUNDER, EAGLE MUM'S KITCHEN

ACTION WEALTH PUBLISHING
www.ActionWealthPublishing.com

Kemp House
152 -160 City Road
London, EC1V 2NX
United Kingdom

ISBN: 978-1-9149-9437-1

Published by Dorine Mwesigwa and Action Wealth Publishing.
Printed and bound in the United Kingdom.

To my beloved parents, Mr. Geddy Mwesigwa and Mrs. Margaret Sanyu Mwesigwa, who gave me the foundation that has brought me this far in life

To my wonderful children, Marcus, Valerie, Melvin, Myles, and Mariah, who allowed me all the time I needed to stay away from them and write this book to completion

To my very special friend, Keith Buswell, who stood by me no matter the storm

CONTENTS

AUTHOR'S NOTE

This book is for anyone who has suffered gut health issues or lack of confidence or self-worth, any child or adult who may have experienced trauma or chronic illnesses of any sort, mood swings, hormonal imbalance, food intolerances, or attention-deficit hyperactivity disorder (ADHD), or if you simply want a better relationship with yourself and others. To better understand yourself and others, this book is for you.

Following on from the premise of the father of modern science Hippocrates, in his statement 2,500 years ago, "All diseases begin in the Gut." Well, with the proof today that *most* diseases begin in the *gut*, it is my belief that the importance of a healthy gut serves optimal health and the overall wellbeing of a person: spiritually, physically, and mentally; mind, body, *and* soul.

My prayers and hopes are that your reading experience will help you to reflect upon your life holistically and inspire you to endeavour to make the necessary changes required, leading to an exciting and healthful total life transformation in all physical, spiritual, and mental aspects of your entire being and existence.

INTRODUCTION

I am Dorine Mwesigwa, and I have always loved food. We met even before I was born, and we've been on a journey ever since. Like every relationship we've had our ups and downs, not just on a scale, but with serious nuances and growth points.

I've always needed food, and I've always needed it to be a certain way. Sadly, like many other couples, I one day, through personal, professional, cultural, and spiritual experiences with nutrition, cooking, and eating, got the gut feeling that it had changed. And when food changes, I change, because we live in a system, so bad changes bring deleterious consequences I simply cannot stomach. *Literally.*

It wasn't the same, natural, salt of the earth, what-you-see-is-what-you-get goodness, transparency, and openness. Soon enough, as life became traumatic and hectic and growing up became a real thing, there was a third, fourth, and hundredth party involved in my relationship with food, bringing their own agendas and coming brazenly and wantonly between us.

When the initial shock, headaches, and hormonal imbalance abated, I looked around to see if anyone else was struggling with their food, too. Through ongoing research, I realised it wasn't a case of the "It's not you, it's me..." that usually accompanies awkward breakups. In fact, across the world, I found that billions of people are living in toxic dietary relationships, either because of dysfunctional dynamics or because our proverbial daily bread has become life-shorteningly toxic. And the worst part is that most of us don't even know the sordid details. Through the pressures of survival and progress, we've started a race often without enough reflection, meaning, and direction, that can catapult us into an early grave.

As I took stock and completed self-assessments, I was able to regain control of my mind, body, and spirit through slowing down and getting back to my roots. And to stems and bulbs and leaves. In my garden, no less! As I stood at the kitchen window, I realised that this adage, "What you're looking so hard for might be staring you right in the face," was truer than I'd dared to admit. Less is more. And despite what our frenetic, rushing-everywhere, capture-Photoshop-post culture deems as progress, simplistic is ultimately holistic. Indeed, if you want your love relationship with food restored, that's the best formula.

We must improve our consciousness around food, healthy ecosystems, food chains from garden to table, and the ritual of eating.

It is in the parts of our lives we work at are where we inevitably see results. It's body and brain science, so, being healthier means today's decisions and actions create our future healthy or unhealthy selves. The ideas shared in this book provide some insights and guidelines—though by no means exhaustive—of the why, what, and how of staying in control of the food that reaches our plates. And we can do it right where we are, right now, even as we take the next bite or sip or plan the next meal or pack a school lunch.

I've always loved cooking, and for me, it's more than filling up. It's a passion, an act of love and charity. It is connection, curiosity culminating in creativity, and new recipes constantly fill my waking thoughts. And apparently, my dreams, too, as I often wake and, seemingly out of nowhere, have some concoction on the brain that I simply have to try out! Not because I'm hungry; but because I know how much my children and those with whom we share it will love the experience. And, of course, there's something priceless about creating something wholesome out of fresh, natural produce and a few herbs and spices. (Some of my favourite recipes are included in this book, too.)

I'm encouraging you to cook and make magic with whatever naturally sourced ingredients you can lay your hands on. Gourmet budget or borderline budget, payday spoils or student allowance, there are options for moving away from harmful processed foods and beverages that may have moved into our lives and bodies without paying rent. It's time to give them notice and set up house with nutrition that actually has your best interests at heart (and your hair and nails and kidneys and so on). You can appreciate the shift that needs to happen. It's a matter of life and death. Cooking for oneself and the transformation that comes with it in a human being's life is an opportunity to get back to basics and live better.

In this book you will learn more about:

❖ The Principle vs. Profit dilemma, some of the scary and stark realities of the misleading strategies of the food industry. The crown of God's creation is involved in a mass experiment for which we never signed up. With this foundation, you can build your personal vitality game plan through informed decisions and just a few small changes.

❖ Getting back to basics and the power of nature, which will help us reverse the damage caused by modern medicine, processed and mass-produced food, and chemicals that have change our growth and ageing processes over time.

❖ Complicated relationships with food that impact childhood development, mental wellness, weight, and a host of lifestyle diseases affecting billions of people across the planet.

❖ The socio-cultural impacts of food, which can provide great insights into the significance of food through sharing, connection, gratitude, and how the meaning of moments can be shaped through communing over a meal or a mere morsel.

❖ The systemic nature of our world, illustrated throughout this book. As with every aspect of an ecosystem, the effects of stress and pressure in the modern world have an interdependent relationship with our food and eating habits.

❖ Food is medicine. The healing properties of the right foodstuffs are explored with examples and natural prescriptions. Many additives and preservatives slowly erode human immunity to the extent that we eventually overmedicate, and it becomes "normal" even for children to go through courses of harmful chemicals. In this book, we consider more viable alternatives.

❖ Rethinking your current food sources and choices, which could literally renew your mind, body, and spirit on a cellular level. This takes conscious self-assessment and committing to taking back control. Turning your patch of land or window-ledge herb garden into a health hub means turning your back on feeling unhealthy, unfit, uncomfortable, and stressed.

There are many routes for renewing your relationship with food, which, for billions, of people is on life support. Mindful practices of cultivating, harvesting, preparing, serving, and enjoying our food completely transforms eating into an experience.

Variety is the spice of life, and culinary creativity and experimentation can be fun and rewarding. There are healthy shortcuts and ingredients we've never tried. The pie is the limit. The pandemic, social distancing, and lockdowns have impacted the way we eat and source food, and hopefully, being indoors offered the opportunity to throw together some delicious treasures. I share some of my favourite Garden to Gut twists and trimmings to the classics.

I strongly believe that food is medicine. In order for us to make any meaningful and sustainable change, we need vision and a heart-resonant reason for doing so. Transformation starts with information and knowledge. I hope this book provides insights and perspectives that will transform your life holistically—your mind, body, and soul, through the natural power of *food*. It has helped me heal from trauma and disease on so many levels. As we look to preserving ourselves and our natural environment, I am excited about the innovative ways that will be generated across the globe.

Join me at the table as we talk realities and recipes, choice and change, and the power of God-given (and well-preserved) sustenance.

To your good health and that of our planet,

Dorine

CHAPTER ONE

CHILDHOOD, SCHOOL AND CAREER

I was born in Uganda on March 19, 1973, in Nsambya Hospital on what was, I'm told, a beautiful Monday morning. I was blessed to be brought up by both my parents, Mr. Geddy Mwesigwa and Mrs. Margaret Mwesigwa. I grew up as one of six, alongside my siblings, Brian, Olga, Trevor, Arnold, and last but not least, Virginia. Ours was a fairly big home family setting, with many animals around: dogs, rabbits, chickens, cats, and some pigeons on the rooftop that appeared and sounded a perpetual feature of our household and my childhood recollections.

My most profound memories growing up are of the two boarding schools I attended. The first one at Namugongo Primary, which brought brand-new experiences, as I was only eleven years old when I left my close-knit family in search of formal education.

Here, I learned how to be independent and to interact with people who were not my close family or relatives.

I made friends very easily, because my default disposition is happy and bubbly. I'm told my love and humour lights up a room as soon as I step inside, and this was evident even as an away-from-home-for-the-first-time little person. It was great meeting new people from different families and backgrounds and with whom there was sufficient grounds for bonding and genuine connection.

Secondary school saw me still as a boarder, this time as a student of Nsambya Saint Joseph's School, also a "girls only" establishment. By this time, I was a fourteen-year-old navigating the stations of self-discovery and exploring my surroundings with a little more knowledge and experience.

My childhood was, for the most part, a happy recollection of playing with just about anything outside. I was an adventurous tomboy with nothing but time on my hands, so my days were filled with sticks and stones, tree climbing, riding bicycles, and most importantly, playing with dolls. Well, *playing* is a mild word, because, at some point, I had broken all my dolls, and before my mother could replace it, I'd made one out of fibre. Necessity spurring on invention and all that, I suppose. My grandmother taught me how to make a fibre doll using a reed growing tall on a banana tree stem (traditionally known as *ebyayi* in my native language).

My peers considered me a tomboy on account of me playing rough all the time. Being the first to scale mango trees and throw the spoils down to my friends was typical. I retained several scars, which I've had to explain to my children many years later, but back then, it was just another day of horseplay. There was no accounting for the adrenaline-induced boisterousness, and I survived constant falls and bruising.

I would come home, and my grandmother would disinfect them with water, after which she would go into the garden and pluck a few leaves of a local plant. Gently heating it in the fire, she would pat my wounds which would invariably sting a bit, but by the following day, the cuts would be dry and healing. I was in awe of Grandma's miraculous powers, which meant I could escape my parent's reprimand and be back in the saddle or branch in under twenty-four hours.

Later, those memories came to help me on my journey back to healing in adulthood. All we need is really within and around us in glorious abundance.

CHILDHOOD: A MIXED BAG AND BREWING RESILIENCE

My formative years brought many critical lessons, inside and beyond the classroom. I rate boarding school highly among those, as the place offered one of the earliest opportunities to shape me, largely because I learned how to do things on my own. It also gave me a sense of freedom, knowing I could be away from the beatings that characterised life at home. Life is always a set of trade-offs. I was leaving the familiar for the foreign, but it also offered a much-needed reprieve from some very real and deep traumas.

Our dad raised us with an iron hand, punishing us with beatings in the name of discipline; not a rod was spared, if it was to make us better people. Every time we did something wrong, even getting bad grades, it unleashed the wrath of "character-building," with scars wholly unrelated to fun, and the adrenaline of racing and tree climbing.

With hindsight, I know he meant well; however, as a child, I interpreted it as hatred. Nevertheless, my tough childhood has made me the resilient and successful person I am today. Considering some harsh realities that brought me to my knees even as an adult, what didn't kill me has fortified me so much and enabled me to bring my family safely through deep waters.

PIVOTAL POINTS AND PERSEVERANCE

There were pivotal points throughout my life that set me on course to grow, course correct, and transform. One significant moment was a risky yet conscious decision to find a job whilst I was still living with my parents and become entirely independent.

During those days, it was very difficult to find work in Uganda, regardless of academic qualifications. So, I would wake each morning and storm the streets of Kampala, going door to door of every office, looking for work. In perfect time, the angels of perseverance smiled down on me kindly, and I landed a job in the first Internet café in Uganda at the time.

The Asian owner had shipped in several computers and sought people with basic computer knowledge skills, which I fortunately possessed, thanks to my dad having taken me to learn basic computer programmes. It was a big thing in Uganda v. Thereafter, I went on to work in four other small up-and-coming Internet cafés. Interestingly enough, I also met my first husband in cyberspace. All the clicking and online searching culminated in marriage. It sounds like a story, but it really happened. It wasn't going to make the Everyman's Guide to Happy Endings list, and the marriage didn't last, but it turned out to be a critical milestone.

Another core learning point came as I completed my Bachelor's degree in Theology, Philosophy, and Religious Studies at the University of Roehampton in South West London. During this time, the global credit crunch coincided with my husband and me stuck at home, jobless. We hatched a plan to return to Germany in search of work, but there was a catch. We needed a house, and without a job, that was next to impossible.

I went online and found properties, called a number, and a German lady speaking very good English told me about a vacant two-bedroom apartment. She asked about my employment and financial viability to pay the rent, and I said, upon our return to Germany, my husband would rejoin his old job of nearly twenty years. We confirmed we wanted to view the apartment as soon as possible, and within five days we had flown to Germany, viewed the living space, and returned to England with a tenancy agreement.

We moved into the apartment the following month with our four kids in tow, and when the shocked agent asked why we never mentioned the children, my husband simply replied, "You never asked." Just like that, on a mere technicality. I found that funny, but it was how we got into another country for a whole new set of experiences.

Life is the ultimate teacher. Perhaps one of the most harrowing lessons came when I finally had to leave Germany and return to the UK. I had established a business that had failed; everything had fallen apart, and I felt with every cell in my body from deep within my gut that I had to push myself, regardless of the prevailing circumstances, and exit the country. Financially, I was in a bad place, not a penny to my name other than a car I had purchased for €8000, two months prior, and a few hundred Euro in the bank.

I went to the housing association, gave them three months' notice on our rental agreement, and went my merry way to start strategizing our departure. I did the same thing as before: went online, found a property agency in the UK (Wolverhampton, to be precise; a friend of mine had told me about big family homes, recently built, to rent in the area), and searched for properties. Within the first ten minutes of my search, I had found exactly what I was looking for and made an appointment to fly into the country and view the house.

I called on the Friday. The following Monday, I flew in and instantly fell in love with the property. I was asked all the same routine vetting questions and advised the agent I'd just shut down my organisation and intended to move back to the UK. This time round, I needed a guarantor who earned more than £40 000. I quickly emailed my brother, who was more than happy to help. Within two weeks, I returned to Germany with a tenancy agreement to sell my car, pack up my belongings and my brood, and embark on this new journey. It turned out the house had been vacant for two years and situated on Eagle Street. [Incidentally, the title of my first book is *Iron Eagle Mum*.] I didn't see this until the day we officially moved in, but it was a clear sign from the universe that this was meant to be.

LESSONS ABOUT EDUCATION

I was always taught to believe that education was the key to my success and I was nothing without it, hence my father took us to the best schools in the country and invested in education more than any other area or aspect of our lives. To him, education was the be-all and end-all of progress and a life worth living.

I subscribed to the idea, too, although his harshness made me rebellious. So much so that I postponed my tertiary studies until I had had all my children. Even as I enjoyed new beginnings and revelled in motherhood, his words persistently haunted me. "Without education, you will never amount to anything of value, and if you are wise, you will pursue your University studies," he said. And, in time, I did.

SCHOOL AND A PROBLEM CHILD

Inasmuch as I was indoctrinated into the virtues of education and managed to achieve the qualifications I desired, school was never really my thing.

When I say "from day one," it's not the proverbial kick-off that we use in common language. The agony and anguish started literally on my first day of kindergarten, when I turned my back to the blackboard. My teacher a British White lady named Mrs. Warren, who was the head teacher, told my mum she had never seen anything like that in all her years of teaching experience. My determined three-year-old self took on (or is it I *turned down?*) the system.

There and then, she started to keep a piercing and relentless eye on me, and it marked the moment I was branded a "problem child." I was difficult and unstable, and thus my school-hopping expedition began. I changed school uniforms, classmates, and teachers very often in the hope (mostly for my parents) that it would better me and get me the grades. It was excruciating, and these perpetual horrors persisted to high school.

My instability in school resulted in constant teasing by other children; on a deep level, I always felt insecure. I grew up without a sense of worth, because no one told me I was (good) enough. Instead, I heard various versions of how everything I did was substandard and that I needed to get better. There was a clear and conditional standard to belonging.

I came to understand later that our bodies keep the score of slights, hurt, and trauma. And it wasn't just in the park or school playground. Even though I never doubt it came from a good place, or perhaps they didn't know any better, but when your closest role models (parents) set you on a path of constant yearning to catch up, this is a slippery downward on the psycho-emotional slope. As this was the standard in my first and most impressionable relationship, I never expected any better from outsiders, which became a really huge challenge.

Despite all that, and with the resolute resilience of the young, I fulfilled many exciting roles along the way. There were memorable and exciting moments with the friends I made and the victories I achieved. Participation on the student council, school sports teams, talent shows, writing competitions, debates, cooking and baking activities, and drama productions ranked among my favourite extracurricular pursuits. I served in leadership roles as class monitor and prefect, and was often selected as the lead role in plays.

As I started reading widely, I learned that I suffered from attention-deficit hyperactivity disorder (ADHD). Symptoms include a short attention span or inattentiveness, hyperactivity and impulsiveness, constant fidgeting, and acting without thinking, all of which showed up in my diagnosis. I learnt more about this condition in Dr. Nadine Burke Harris's *The Deepest Well: Healing the Long-Term Effects of Childhood Adversity*.

She goes on to explain how exposure to childhood trauma in high doses affects brain development, immune system and hormonal systems, and even the way our DNA is read and transcribed. It was profoundly insightful. The trauma can be so severe and pervasive that it causes threats that get under our skin and affect our entire physiology. This includes events like abuse or neglect or even growing up with a parent battling mental illness or substance dependence. In my case, the trauma emanated from growing up with a parent whose belief that sparing the rod meant spoiling the child had led him to mete out persistent violent discipline.

Needless to say, the effects of these traumas followed me into adult relationships and issues of wellbeing.

Key Highlights

* Certificate in Cookery and Culinary training August 2021
* Author, *Iron Eagle Mum,* published 2017
* University of Bonn, Germany, October 2014-October 2015
* University of Roehampton, London, September 2011-April 2014

Sacred Pursuits

I remain profoundly passionate about the things of God and spirituality; initially, they set me on my academic path of studying theology.

I wanted to know God for myself from an academic perspective, as I had already experienced Him on a spiritual level. I was curious to know what the great philosophers and theologians had to say about the Word of God, the Bible. I firmly and deeply believe that God is all things good, which has guided me as an author and a Life Transformational Coach.

Both of these pursuits provided me a vehicle to serve others through sharing my story. Through reflection on some key life lessons, I wanted to use my experiences as an example, so others could see themselves making similar experiences and know that, even though they've been through the worst, redemption and success are our portion. I am called to love and serve others for the glory of God, and the more I reflected on this, the more ways I found to help others in simple and complex ways. Even sharing my own journey with releasing trauma and getting back to the ground and the garden has helped so many people rethink their daily choices and actions.

I am greatly inspired by Oprah Winfrey, because her story resonates so much with mine in all aspects. The most fun and amazing part is that, against all odds, she survived and became a super-success and global icon. More than that, she lived not only to tell her story but also to inspire others through her work, hence touching millions of lives across the world, people who, in turn, can learn from her inspiration and relate that to others.

PROFESSIONAL PATHS, PASSION, AND PROBLEM-SOLVING

Our experience adds up. My having worked in a variety of settings brought me a broad-based perspective and many interests.

During my stay in Germany, I volunteered in a kitchen at a nursing home, where I helped prepare food for the elderly. Caring for the residents was fun and fulfilling, but what I didn't realise at the time, while stacking the trays and trolleys, was that I would eventually study the culinary arts.

Starting out my career, I was instrumental in establishing the first up-and-coming Internet café in Kampala, Uganda and worked at four others, thereafter holding the positions of accountant and director. This helped me to understand business and evolve offerings, as social and economic impacts often necessitated unforeseen change.

For the most part, though, I've always preferred working for myself. My first business was a small kiosk in my home area, Nsambya Estate, selling basic household essentials. Thereafter, I started a small business selling secondhand shoes by going door to door, from people's homes to offices and different workplaces. I later established a Life Transformational Coaching business whilst in Germany, and upon returning to the UK, I established the same.

My greatest and most rewarding job, however, has been motherhood. Raising my children has been by far my main role, and everything I do is around them. Hence, I've worked from home for most of my career. My greatest pride stems from the fact that I have been, and still am, a committed mother against all the odds. And believe me, there were times when the scales were tipped to a nerve-wracking degree.

My priceless treasures are embodied in two daughters and two sons: Valerie, 18, Melvin, 17, Myles, 12, and Mariah, 11. I raised very respectable, respectful, kind, caring, intelligent, loving, talented, God-fearing children, regardless of whatever we've experienced as a family. Their courage and perseverance shine through in their school grades, interactions with their peers and others in general, and also through their many talents and gifts.

Naturally, there were challenges, as working for oneself has never been easy. My first two businesses went well, and I progressed from the first to a second, more rewarding one. However, I have had to close down some operations due to economic downturn and issues surrounding the COVID-19 pandemic.

My career path has been very helpful in leading me to where I am now, because it has everything to do with love, service, and compassion to others. That is exactly what the Bible says: "Love thy brother as you love yourself." And that is what the study of theology has also shown me.

There are some characteristics that helped me in my coaching business and many other people-centred roles.

I am a good listener, and this creates a space for clients to explore their experiences from different perspectives. However, being a good listener has also worked to my detriment, at times, as I tend to take on many people's problems. I constantly have to erect and maintain healthy boundaries, so I can pour from a full cup.

Most recently, I changed direction and, in getting back to basics, qualified in a basic culinary cooking experience. This proved so inspiring that I decided to start teaching the rediscovered secrets contained in the magic of even the most basic sustenance. I can lose myself in the wonderland of my kitchen, rustling up recipes from scratch or adding an Iron Eagle Mum twist on the classics. Cooking is sharing, sustenance, and service, and remains one of my all-time favourite ways to show the people I love just how much.

RELATIONSHIPS AND TRAUMA

I've been married twice; however, both marriages were nullified.

I met my first husband online, when I was in Uganda and he based in the UK. The on-screen romance blossomed, and I later joined him, and we got married. The bliss did not last long, though, as I didn't have much appetite for an abusive.

I met my second husband in a pub across the road from my house. He had travelled from Germany and was on holiday in the area for a couple of weeks. He crossed over to the table where I sat and asked if I cared to play a game of pool with him. Not too interested, I reluctantly agreed. We played the game, and at the end of the night, while saying our goodbyes, he joked that he would stop over at my place in the morning for a coffee. Again, I reluctantly went along with it, and he made good on his promise.

A year later, we were married; a few years of bliss ended abruptly, though, as something truly unspeakable caused our separation. He had sexually abused my four children for the five years he took care of them, while I pursued my university studies. This initiated a journey of introspection, healing, and release. If my children and I were to grow up restored and realising the God-breathed purpose and potential inherent in each and every one of us, we had to go down an essential, restorative path together.

PRECIOUS MOMENTS AND HEAVEN ON EARTH

From the good times and the hard times, I've learned to take nothing for granted. Life is precious and, if COVID is anything to go by, shorter than we realise. My best times are with my family: meal times, school events, holidays, cooking together, movie nights, pillow fights, gardening as a family, shopping, all the extracurricular activities, and so much more give me cause for humbling gratitude. All we have and all we are is grace and mercy, and when I look at my children, in particular, I feel the surge of powerful surrender.

I've learned better balance through a conscious decision to be congruent, persistent, consistent, and authentic at all times in all that I do. Like bad margarine on bad bread, I've learned not to spread myself too thin and instead to engage in things that align to my purpose.

My values guide my resolutions to do more through discipline, patience, efficiency, compassion, kindness, love, and service. Rewiring the narrative of not being good enough, I've traded elusive perfection for excellence.

STAPLE INGREDIENTS THAT SUSTAIN ME

Life offers each of us a buffet, and it demands a discerning palate. Through trial, error, and transformation, we can make better choices.

Through my experiences, I've selected some staples that sustain me along this journey of life. I have learnt to believe, even when I don't yet know the outcome of any circumstance. My faith has come as a result of listening to my gut; hence, I lead from the heart and not only from the head.

I have come to recognise that *fear* is the thief of all joy. All the risks I've taken demonstrate that I have overcome fear, because I know on the other side of fear is something so striking and unimaginably beautiful.

I've learnt that life will throw anything at you, most of it without warning sign. What's important is not to resist any situation but to go with the flow, regardless of the circumstances. Easier said than done as it may sound, I believe it's the best way to navigate life. I believe, no matter what, there is a higher power that knows everything, and He intends well for me in all things. A victim mentality cannot sprout from such experiences.

LIFE HAPPENS *FOR* ME, NOT *TO* ME

I have learnt that the power of forgiveness is one of the most powerful tools and gifts we have or can give to ourselves. I have learnt that the past is gone, the future is not here yet, and all we have is the Now. For this reason, I live in the moment and enjoy and appreciate it for every ounce it has to give.

I have learnt the power of having an attitude of gratitude. There are times of dearth, and then there are times of bounty; both afford us lessons in thankfulness and perspective.

I have learnt that *love* is our ultimate goal in this life. The Bible says, "Above all, love each other deeply, because love covers over a multitude of sins." (1 Peter 4:8)

These values have guided me like a global positioning system, steering me through life so I do not repeat my mistakes. I love that I am nevertheless still a work in progress.

CHAPTER TWO

TAKING STOCK

Food for Thought: How our Diets Compare to Previous Generations

Through the nuances of my food journey, I periodically take stock of how we're doing. Our diets and that of our parents and grandparents are quite different, and health issues that people today are experiencing in their twenties and thirties were unheard of fifty or so years ago.

Some pertinent themes became apparent:

- ❖ Urbanization has been a major force in global obesity.

- ❖ Overweight and obesity issues emerged in low- and middle-income countries; hunger and malnutrition were no longer the only critical issues in these demographics.

❖ Away-from-home eating and changes in edible oil production created by cheap vegetable oils allowed low- and middle-income countries to increase energy consumption at very low income levels.

WE ARE WHAT WE EAT, AND WE'RE CHANGING AS A SPECIES

Extensive research shows that, over the past several decades, a dramatic shift in how the entire globe eats, drinks, and moves has clashed with our biology to create major shifts in body composition.[1]

From this study, we note how the prevalence of overweight people and obesity was estimated to afflict nearly 1.5 billion adults worldwide in 2008, which later proved an undercount. It predicts that, in 2030, an estimated 2.16 billion adults globally will be overweight, and 1.12 billion will be obese. The implications hereof for health, quality of life, productivity, and healthcare costs are mind-boggling, and the greatest risks are for much of Asia, Latin America, the Middle East, and Africa.

RITUALS, DISCIPLINES, AND ROUTINES

Chances are our grandparents followed a stricter routine than some of us do. It was typical for a family to have their meals at the same time every day, and their

---

[1] www.ncbi.nlm.nih.gov/pmc/articles/PMC3257829/.

bodies became accustomed to knowing when to expect food. This discipline helped waistlines stay slim and limited food wastage.

In modern times, however, our work and life schedules are often hit and miss. Skipping breakfast, grazing or snacking, and several cups of coffee a day would've been foreign ideas to our forebearers.

Globalisation brought changes in the availability and nature of work and entrepreneurship. Instead of standard hours or shift work, the modern world offers 24/7 products and services around the globe, so people work odd hours and are "switched on" most of the time. Remote work, made more prevalent through the COVID-19 pandemic, also means we're sitting down for hours on end in virtual meetings or reading or typing. We're often not even registering the food we eat as we push to meet a deadline or clear our Inbox. Snacking and convenience meals often mean more gets done with fewer dishes to wash! A more sedentary lifestyle, of course, means we're consuming more calories than we use, so exercise, breaks, and spending time in nature are even more critical for vitality.

Decades ago, learning to cook was the surest way to goodness on your plate, and it was most often done by a woman in the house. I remember a Zimbabwean colleague once telling me that her neighbour's daughter was sent back home on a bus with a three-legged pot, minus her dowry and husband, when her mother-in-law figured out she couldn't cook. There was embarrassment and shame for days as the word spread and her bridegroom watched her leave the village then returned to his mother's home-cooked recipes. I'm not judging; just reporting. I'm not making a point about who should be cooking, because I know of a number of single dads who raise their children with little support. More, I am showing how cooking was something that we focused on, back in the day.

These days, cooking has become more of a hobby rather than a necessity, and many people can't recognise one kitchen implement from another. Where there is no time, passion, or often a helper or support system, convenience meals become enticing. Simple innovations like refrigeration mean that there's less need to plant crops and do daily shopping.

It's definitely not as complicated as it looks, and even delicious healthy meals don't have to cook all day like before. We can now choose to go back to basics and self-sufficiency. It doesn't have to be a limited repertoire, either, as you will discover throughout this book or through the thousands of online resources available. The most renowned chefs are consciously bringing healthy options to the table as they partner with organisations to beat lifestyle diseases and enhance vitality and balance.

Back then, it was probably a set weekly menu with specific meal days. All the leftovers could be used up, served with fresh vegetables every night. What they lacked in variety, they made up in easily prepared meals and regular servings of nutritious vegetables.

Today, we are besieged by bucketloads of options. Foods are prepared, served, and eaten differently, and fast food has become a pandemic. Yesterday's leftovers may not be as appealing as some franchise's "secret" recipe for fried chicken or steak grilled along the street. A microwave meal or an instant just-add-water shake is quicker than chopping a fruit salad or stir fry. Instead of eating at a table, we often slump in front of the television or computer. Eating in the car as we rush to an appointment has become normalised. We now have the allure of convenience (eating a tin of out-of-season fruit) or 24/7 drive-through outlets or if-it's-late-it's-free, store-to-door delivery service, but *what is the cost?*

Concept restaurants offer experiences many take for granted. Back in the day, it was a rare treat to have a meal out, but these days "family restaurant" franchises offer a diverse menu, free WIFI (we ask at the door), and connection points for devices, while the children play safely with a minder. They have specials for different days, and soon it becomes a regular haunt; often, we spend hours with everyone at the table on their mobile phone. The service isn't always great, and the prices often don't justify the dining experience, but it can easily become part of our routine.

On the plus side, more information is available about food than 60 years ago. There is ongoing research and programmes available to create healthy, nutrient-based meal plans.

SCIENTIFIC ADVANCEMENTS

With the Industrial Revolution came new technologies and processes that changed the way people lived, worked, ate, and engaged. Through scientific advancements came experimentation and the invention of manmade chemicals that made their way into our food supply across the ecosystem. Food preservation, mass production, and genetic modification became the vehicles for enormous profits.

The food industry soon enough realized it could extend the shelf life of basic produce, resulting in prepacked and overprocessed food (and I use the word loosely), laden with additives, colourants, enhancers. Over the last sixty years, over 10, 000 food additives have been created for use. These do not improve the quality of food, and very few have the health benefits that advertising and marketing promises; instead, as subsequent sections will show, they are very harmful.

There are more illnesses today and many didn't exist six decades ago; with the invention of such medications as antibiotics, we now are dealing with serious infections, but also killing off microbes. Our natural biochemical balance is disrupted, and our self-regulating and healing capacity destroyed. Our health quality today has dropped tremendously, compared to people who lived fifty or so years ago, who were not exposed to many of these medications; back then, they mostly depended on food for healing.

One of the greatest impacts on our food sourcing has been the transition from farms into massive industrial factories designed to raise, contain, and slaughter animals as efficiently and cheaply as possible. Today, roughly 94% of all animals raised for human consumption spend their lives on these huge factory farms, and the conditions have come under concerned scrutiny by animal activists and climate scientists.

Humans have been experimenting with selection and manipulation of crops strains throughout civilisation, but the 1970s took this to a whole new level with genetically engineered crops. This brought a reprieve from the swarms of locusts and other plagues that destroyed entire harvests, but the resulting herbicides and pesticides bring their own dangers.

Some food trends have come full circle. From organic to mass production and back to organic and regenerative agriculture; from farm stalls to hypermarkets and back to glamorised fresh-food market franchises making billions of dollars, as consumer education increases healthy eating, climate change, pollution, environmental degradation, and eliminating bad habits, all at exorbitant costs.

In Poor Taste: Mass Production, Sugarcoating, Genetic Modification, and Fine Print

It's so uncanny that something as vital as food and eating should be this confusing and controversial, but perhaps the very fact that we need it as often as we do for survival has prompted industry players towards consumer exploitation. My message throughout this book is for us to take control through knowledge and plausible and credible sources and to become our own nutritionist or food specialist, eating and drinking what is naturally available for optimal health.

It's not so much about budget (even as malnutrition and poverty are stark realities) or what we're in the mood for; it is more about knowing what's *inside* the pretty packaging or what's being punted on social media.

Having read widely (by no means exhaustively), it's a very scary menu we're facing. There is also conscious intent to mask from the average consumer the real and life-threatening dangers. We need to think about the entire life cycle and value chain; lifestyle diseases, most of which are preventable; when and how much we eat and what we put on our plates; and more importantly, how we socialise our children around food, nutrition, and wellness from the earliest age.

I was fascinated by the contribution of Vani Hari, noted as one of the Most Influential People on the Internet by *Time* magazine, the *New York Times* best-selling author of *The Food Babe Way and Feeding You Lies: How to Unravel the Food Industry's Playbook and Reclaim Your Health,* and co-founder of Truvani. She is a food activist (who would've imagined we would ever need such a role?). Through aggressive corporate activism, petitioning, and impactful social media campaigns, Hari and her Food Babe Army have become one of the most powerful populist forces in the health and food industries.

Her studies and findings highlight how food companies and manufacturers, often endorsed by experts, manipulate nutrition research; how fake news fuels feeding habits; how they make their food addictive (even that sold in health food stores); how organic and free-range are not as safe as initially touted; how damaging ingredients are hidden through inconsistent and partial oversight; and how the landmines of food politics are brought to our lips with harrowing consequences.[2] Through her relentless efforts, she's gotten huge corporations to remove some of the most harmful ingredients from popular foods. Let's get to know more about these fine print foes.

FOOD ADDITIVES

It turns out science is not all that dedicated to sustaining healthy living in all aspects. Money and greed still find roots to create profit over ethical food practices.

A few years ago, Hari campaigned for the Subway franchise to remove a chemical called azodicarbonamide (when heated, it turns carcinogenic), which had been banned all over the globe. They weren't using it in other countries but persisted with it in their bread in American outlets.

Just to give you a sense, this is the same chemical used in rubber and yoga mats. It's the element in the exercise mat that creates the evenly dispersed air bubbles, which was the same property they wanted in their bread. It was one way to ensure their bread rolls were uniform across all their stores. But obviously, this is a hazardous chemical not necessary in our food and providing risks to the consumer.

---

[2] https://mariamarlowe.com/podcast/lies-the-food-industry-feeds-us-with-vani-hari/.

There are also a number of chemicals invented to mimic the taste of naturally occurring foodstuffs, which are added to foods created in a laboratory. This has impacted for our brain chemistry and how we register satiety and nutritional adequacy. Yeast extract and MSG, for example, are added to many items and can even be found in organic food.

MSG is monosodium glutamate, which is essentially salt plus glutamate, and it creates that (fake) flavour in your mouth, leading to your mouth watering as you continue to crave a flavour. Food manufacturers have figured out they can replace monosodium glutamate with yeast extract, which is that glutamate. So, the ingredient lists look fairly roadworthy, but then they add salt separately and still create the same kind of flavour profile that creates addiction to the taste.

This explains our overeating things that superficially taste good, but which render very little to zero nutritional value. This can happen with the usual suspects of high-carb snacks like crisps and crackers, but it has also been found in gluten-free, vegan, or organic alternatives that are considered healthier and often very pricey. There, too, it becomes easy to scarf down entire family-sized bags of treats without even noticing.

Another common threat is the effects of pesticides and herbicides used to protect crops. From this came a campaign for non-GMO foods everywhere. The majority of GMO foods we eat actually come from seeds that were patented to withstand heavy doses of Roundup a powerful weed-killer. The seeds survive, and thus the actual harvests of corn, soy, and canola still contain traces of this toxic chemical, glyphosate.

We look out for non-GMO project-verified products, because they do not derive from a genetically engineered crop, but there is still room for a technicality. Compliance dictates that 95% of the ingredients in that product cannot be sourced from any non-GMO crops, but they still can come from conventional crops *sprayed* with the very same herbicides we're trying to avoid.

Investigations have also surfaced that many scary elements lurk in that 5%. As an example, oats, in many locations, are pre-harvested with Roundup, a chemical herbicide that the World Health Organization and the International Agency for Research Lung Cancer have found to be a probable carcinogen, through identifying its main ingredient called glyphosate. It's safer to grow your own produce and buy from reputable suppliers.

Do you speak Organic?

As consumer knowledge increases along with many ailments, allergens, and inflammation, there is a rising trend back to basics, including free-range and organic. But here again, it's helpful to know the fine print.

A product could be labelled *100% Organic.* That means every single ingredient is organic and hasn't been sprayed with anything synthetic. It is important that our food is organic, but also *non-GMO.*

In addition, upon careful investigation you may find that natural flavours, yeast extract, or carrageenan sneak into some certified organic products. Oftentimes, organic food producers and stores and manufacturers endeavour to reproduce popular treats and meals in healthier, less allergic ways, but they include various additives, as well. There is a list of permissible ingredients. Carrageenan, an emulsifier often linked to bloating, gut irritation, and lowered immunity, is *not* on that list and prohibited from inclusion in organic foods.

When food is labelled *Organic* (vs. *100% Organic*), it is often made with 70% organic ingredients and 30% chemical landmines or anything else. Chocolate and some energy bars often contain non-organic soy protein isolate, for example, which is also troublesome.

DANGEROUS AND SHINY THINGS

When the same chemical appears on the label of your favourite hot drink *and* on your luggage, there must be a problem! You're clearly going nowhere fast other than to the grave, with your steaming cocoa in hand.

Hari started her company, Truvani® (www.truvani.com), to create products that were "real foods without chemicals—Products without chemicals; labels without lies." Her inspiration was to develop protein powers and other health supplements that were compliant with California's Proposition 65, a law that requires businesses to provide warnings to Californians about significant exposures to chemical that cause cancer, birth defects, or other reproductive harm. While these warnings can be in homes or workplaces or pertain to chemicals released into the environment, she looked at products that Californians purchase, notably in the health and wellness arena.

There are numerous contaminants found in food and commercial health supplements, starting with heavy metals like lead, arsenic, cadmium, mercury, and others. Food safety guidelines dictate particular thresholds, and where a product exceeds it, the manufacturer is required to add a Prop 65 warning label. Extensive testing is needed to ensure safety levels, and not every manufacturer goes the distance, so this an important area of development. As consumers, we can only be aware and check our food labels.

Colourants such as the products used in Coca-Cola and Pepsi often end up in gourmet coffees. So, your commitment to get off bad, sugary soft drinks could send you toward coffee, but the dangerous chemicals are loitering just under the foamy coffee art in a cappuccino or latte. Often swopping out a greasy burger leads you to a salad, but then you need to read the label on shop-bought salad dressings and vinaigrettes.

OBLITERATING IMMUNITY

A rushed and pressured lifestyle can seriously compromise the human immune system, which is the body's mechanism for fighting off contractable illnesses and infections.

Diet plays a significant role in human and animal immunity. Scientific research shows us how the compounds and elements in food can either enhance or damage our metabolic arsenal. Diets high in added sugar and surplus salt are linked to increased risk of inflammation, certain autoimmune conditions, and several chronic diseases.[3] While not all inflammatory and immune conditions (including obesity and Type 2 diabetes) are caused by the diet, since environmental disruptions, medication, and genetics also factor in, it is helpful to steer clear of the high-risk foods and drinks.

Processed foods contain unhealthy fats, sugars, and additives. These foods taste better and may last longer, but they also may weaken the immune system. Tinned

---

[3] www.medicalnewstoday.com/articles/foods-that-weaken-immune-system.

foods, microwaveable and ready-meals, and high-carb snacks like chips and biscuits are among the main offenders.

Also, check the labels for additives such as sucralose, aspartame, carboxymethylcellulose, polysorbate 80, sodium, and carrageenan; they are all associated with inflammation. Research abounds on the relationship between diets high in additives (e.g., emulsifiers, thickeners, and sweeteners), sugars, and refined fats and resultant obesity, immune-related inflammation, and concomitant insulin resistance. A 2014 study illustrated how the intake of salt, refined sugar, saturated fat, and omega-6 fatty acids, along with a shortage of omega-3 fatty acids, can damage the immune system.

Diets high in refined sugar bring an increased risk for chronic conditions, such as coronary heart disease and Type 2 diabetes. As much as we may enjoy store-bought preserves and sweets, flavoured milk and other sweetened dairy products, juices, and sodas, they essentially sabotage our immune system. Sugar, while also being incredibly addictive (often compared to the addictive powers of drugs) reduces the effectiveness of white blood cells, which causes inflammation. It is important to check food labels, as refined sugar is added to items you wouldn't expect, such as bread or tinned beans.

Fried and fast food compromise immunity, as they increase gut permeability and bacterial imbalance in the gut.[4] The bottom line is that we need to get good-food savvy and create our own mix of palatable and sustainable vitality.

We can't talk food issues without touching on the impact of antibiotics, which make their way into our commercialised meat products. Antibiotics or antibacterials are medications formulated to target bacterial infections such as urinary tract, sinus, or ear infections. Prior to 1936 when the first manmade antibiotics were used, thirty percent of all deaths resulted from bacterial infections.[5]

Penicillin, the first chemical antibiotic, was in fact discovered by accident. It had been growing from a mass of mould on a petri dish. It turns out a certain type of fungus naturally produced penicillin. Eventually, the fungus was used to produce huge quantities of penicillin in a laboratory. Some other forms of antibacterials were produced by ground soil bacteria.

Antibiotics bring their own share of side effects (natural alternatives are covered in later chapters), but they are also powerful medications that work very well

---

[4] www.healthline.com/nutrition/foods-that-weaken-immune-system#1.-Added-sugar.

[5] www.healthline.com/health/how-do-antibiotics-work.

for certain serious types of afflictions. They are becoming less potent these days, however, because of the increase in antibiotic resistance. This condition occurs when bacteria can no longer be controlled or destroyed by certain forms of antibiotics. In effect, this then means there are no effective treatments for certain medical conditions.

Research shows that, annually, around two million people are infected with antibiotic-resistant bacteria, resulting in more than 20,000 deaths. By 2050, some researchers predict that antibiotic resistance will result in 10 million deaths each year, surpassing cancer as the leading cause of mortality worldwide.[6] The abuse of antibiotics for personal medication and certain agricultural production practices creates a great risk for developing and maintaining immunity.

The meat industry is notorious for adding routine antibiotics in meat production. The demands of the meat industry severely strain the health of animals. Farming animals for meat is a particularly intense process, with limited recovery time between births (e.g., pigs), which compromises their immune system. Living in confined spaces also increases the risk of diseases spread to one another and to humans.

---

[6] www.medicalnewstoday.com/articles/323639#Implications-for-human-health

Antibiotics are also used as growth promoters, even though this practice has been banned in many countries, including the US, China and the European Union; however, there are still some flying under the radar. The preventative use of antibacterials means that some farmers feed it to animals whether they are sick or not. *Read more on this in later chapters, to understand the impact of a healthy ecosystem.*

Animal antibiotics impact human biology through the consumption of antibiotic residues in meat, which creates a bacterial imbalance in the gut (even though the risk is deemed very low in certain countries). The theory is that, in both organic or non-organic agricultural practices, there is a withdrawal period during which antibiotics are stopped to clear the system, before an animal is milked or killed or meat. This, too, will require very stringent oversight from relevant authorities.

LACK OF OVERSIGHT

Due to the efforts of many food activists and an increasing level of consumer awareness, food manufacturers have been pressured to add warning labels to their packaging. For example, there is sufficient evidence that certain artificial food dyes have detrimental effects on children's activity and attention. Dyes made from petroleum and synthetic chemicals have been shown to precipitate hyperactivity in children. These are the kinds of things that should be declared and visible. Unfortunately, some global manufacturers will remove harmful additives in countries where they are regulated and yet continue to use it in locations without oversight.

Research has shown that governments do not control the food and beverage industries to necessary levels, and in the US, there are shocking statistics where toxic substances are added to foods, but this is not reported. Of the 10,000 known additives, only around 3,000 are highlighted. There are products with as many as 100 ingredients on the label; even the most aware consumer won't spend the time reading chemicals and manufacturing details they're not knowledgeable about. An easier option? Choose foods with fewer ingredients; *Less Is More*. Michael Pollan suggests even 15 ingredients per product requires a pause.

"Don't eat anything your great grandmother wouldn't recognise as food," he says. "When you pick up that box of portable yoghurt tubes or eat something with fifteen ingredients you can't pronounce, ask yourself what those things are doing there ... Don't eat anything with more than five ingredients or ingredients you can't pronounce"[7]

---

[7] Pollan, Michael. *In Defense of Food.* New York, Penguin Press, 2008.

Ideally, if the food was just the food, such as a fruit, vegetable, or free-range animal humanely slaughtered, there would be only one ingredient!

Of course, marketing plays a huge role in where consumers spend their hard-earned cash. The packaging, the advertising (have you seen the happy, vibrant family narratives playing out to sell sugar and preservative-laden kiddies' cereals?) focusing on *calories* or *low-fat* or *kilojoules per serving* or *organic* takes us away from the fine print; then, we believe we are making smarter choices when, in fact, our decisions may be made on incomplete data. Food is one of the most marketed items on Earth, so exploitation is a given.

There is a dangerous misconception that just because something is in print or endorsed by certain experts or enjoys a social media following, then it's the truth. And since we often spend more time scrolling through the feeds and not always intentionally investigating, we settle on a food truth and swear by it for a long time. The truth is you will have to be your own food and nutrition investigator and use your own (and your family's) health and wellness as the most credible data.

THE CURSE OF FOOD ADDICTION

If you've ever eaten something "small" or just taken in "a little snack," only to find you've finished the entire thing and are ready to dump the packaging, you've met the potency of addiction.

Somewhere between willpower and a laboratory lies the path to poor digestion, poor physical and mental functioning, and an insatiable hunger that we were not born with. It's manmade, scientifically researched, superbly orchestrated, and insanely profitable. And it comes without a warning sign. Some food manufacturers add innocuous substances like "natural flavours" or MSG additives and others that create a specific trigger in the brain. You remember a flavour, recalling a particular taste and can't stop eating it. When the packaging convinces you it's healthy, or if you're so engrossed in work or a task that you're simply chewing mindlessly, you will continue eating and eventually stock up on these products.

Our biology and chemistry inevitably change over time, and we choose these options that often don't keep us full long enough, while steering away from healthy and natural alternatives. Our palates become used to the oversalted, artificially flavoured foods, sauces, and condiments.

The food giants furthermore figured out they can use these added flavours to mass-processed fare or include processed chemicals in "not close to real" food, so it tastes like real food. It's poisoning with a sizeable side order of profit. Our constantly switched-on and everything-on-the-run lifestyles make this almost too easy.

Part of our tradition has always been porridge, cooked in different yet wholesome ways, as a staple. Oat and oatmeal, wheat, maize, millet, sorghum, rice, and such variants were cultivated, harvested, and served with minimum fuss and zero additives. When anything gets to a shelf, however, it needs boosters (additives and preservatives) that can keep them on there for months and years. Compliments of post-Industrial Revolution innovations, even milk can stay in a box, away from a fridge, for months without going off. But perhaps that "long life" proposition is a misleading misnomer and a contradiction in fine-printed terms.

A popular trend is instant oats with a variety of interesting, almost healthy sounding, flavours. For those seeking an adventurous start to the day, there are oats with bananas and cream, strawberry, or caramel flavourings added to what is still believed to be a staple. Some other brands like Jungle Oats sell them in boxes of ten varieties, and on paper or on the shelf, this looks like a pretty easy way to get through a week and a half of breakfasts or snacks. They, too, have a strawberries-and-cream variety. The consumer can immediately imagine that oats are a great source of slow-release nourishment with the added bonus of fibre to support digestion, and of course strawberries are not as stodgy or sugary as a banana, so it's probably not too bad an option.

Vani Hari investigated the strawberries-and-cream variety of Quaker Instant Oats, a popular and convenient just-add-water sachet that you can carry and prepare wherever. She found that "strawberries" were, in actual fact, just dried apples modified to look like strawberries with natural and artificial flavouring added, to create that pop in your brain that makes you think you're eating real strawberries. So, no nutrients or antioxidant properties from strawberries in the mix anywhere, but your brain chemically registers that it's eating real strawberries.

Then comes the challenge: at some point, it triggers that it isn't enjoying a real fruit, because the nutrition isn't forthcoming, so it forges a path to find it somewhere else. And then comes the Craving Caveat: you now want something else and consume more food than you should or intended to; over time, these cravings hijack your tastebuds, cells, and entire body. And that's just breakfast! This happens with foodstuffs across the pantry and shopping cart; and these natural flavours (look out for them on the ingredients list) also sneak into our snacks and treats. Soon enough, everything else tastes bland and flat, right up to the point when you start a conscious detox and reboot your system completely.

Refining and processing food breaks it down until it has a greater surface area, which in turn causes spikes in blood sugar levels. Processing also decreases nutrients. We should be eating to feed our bodies, not ruin it

The good news, of course, is that you can reverse some of the damage in only a few weeks. Chances are, if you're going to take a few extra minutes to bake your own confectionary with reputable and natural ingredients, you'll have a few and feel sated. The ones in the fancy packaging are more likely to see you get to the bottom of the packet or tin sooner than you intended and, moments later, planning your next meal.

These natural flavours are also in health food shops, which are often more expensive and inspire a sense of being on the right side of the wellness track. Research reveals that, when we eat nutrient-rich real food, our bodies experience all the biochemical reactions normally experienced when we feel full. This doesn't happen with chemically modified food, so we start rationalising buying these derailers in bulk or cashing in on sales without due consideration of the long-term metabolic impact.

Diets have fashions and trends as much as clothes and shoes. High-profile celebrities and doctors often endorse these endeavours. Fat was bad, and now it's good. Grains were good, and then came gluten-free and wheat-free. Sugar-free and sweeteners high in chemicals were never going to be good, but we only learned that later. Coconut oil was a miracle mix, until it wasn't. From the struggle with obesity, other lifestyle and mental issues, we often opt for a quick fix or a miracle programme, some quite pricey, only to find that it produces another set of unintended risks and consequences.

Low-carb-high-protein, Intermittent Fasting, Banting, Paleo, Military, Atkin's, and thousands of others, along with tape measures and tracking apps, are rendering millions desperate and wreaking havoc with their systems, while food corporations are making trillions of dollars annually. And often, after failed attempts, while we figure out what will really work, we're having that "farewell" slice of cake as we bid an unconvincing farewell to the bad eating habits. With our crumbs and food-based allergies, we set about changing for the better. But what is that "better" for each of us as individuals?

With socio-economic advancements and globalisation, certain levels of African society are getting closer to the issues that the US, Europe, and countries like Australia have been grappling with for decades. Fast-food chains are becoming a way of life, and with online ordering and fast delivery, the dangers are coming to our doors.

The good news is that knowledge acted on is power, and you can select whole foods and options that are non-processed and packaged and that won't take ten minutes to get through the ingredients list. With online grocery shopping, chances are the ingredients won't be checked at all, so become even more vigilant. A greasy takeaway meal and a tin of something seemingly innocent could hold the same risk!

EASY MEAL REVOLUTION: CONVENIENCE AT THE CLICK OF A BUTTON

Technology advancement and the explosion of e-Commerce in the early 2000s quickly saw increases in avenues for food sales and delivery. So much so, that traditional corner shops, supermarkets, and restaurant outlets and franchises regard store-to-door delivery a huge competitive advantage and area for innovation. Much of the impetus stems from socio-cultural issues, such as growth in urban populations, increased standards of living and disposable income, consumerism and the desire for options, an instant-gratification culture, marketing savvy, and an increase of working women.

With much to do, it is often easier for some to order food online. With a plethora of food apps and the allure of loyalty rewards, consumers are spoilt for choice among thousands of fast-food and even healthy food suppliers. Home chefs working with reliable delivery services offer more options, as well. The challenge is not so much about getting a meal conveniently with easy payment platforms, but perhaps more about the quality and nutritional value of the food and the hygiene standards of the establishment and transport service.

The global COVID-19 pandemic fundamentally altered our relationship with food: what, where, why, when, and how we eat. I'm interested to see how this impacts us over the next few decades. The mental and physical challenges of the pandemic and regulations to prevent the spread of the virus meant that millions of us were stuck indoors, some bored, lonely, anxious, or frustrated. And those who could, ate.

The pandemic hugely expedited the convenience click-for-food culture. Just about anything can be delivered to our doors in the shortest possible time. Convenience and (relative) safety are key offerings as more people work remotely and many schools battle disrupted schedules. As this is perhaps a long-term possibility, we must consider the impact of a sedentary lifestyle, food addiction, and loss of social capital experiences such as engaging outside the home or anticipating a special occasion away from the couch. It can easily become habit-forming to order takeaways when your profile is set, account details are pre-loaded and the app algorithms eventually send you reminders and a new special every day, as Smartphone technology and Artificial Intelligence are bound to do.

Our world never sleeps. You can do your banking, buy a home, or order a hotdog 24/7. Our young children are technology natives, and they use it for anything and everything. We must support them to make healthy food choices and not get sucked into the often insular "click and collect" (at the front door) culture.

SOCIAL MEDIA AND SUSTENANCE

There is such a thing as food photography and a phenomenon known as food porn. I didn't know this ten years ago. Back then, I cooked, prayed, ate, chatted, and cleared the dishes. But in time, I recognised that we eat with our eyes, and presentation has an impact on our eating experience.

One article reported more than 400 million posts tagged #food and 250 million tagged #foodporn on Instagram. This is the extent to which social media users are inundated with visual displays of food.[8] Buzzfeed's *Tasty* has become the world's largest digital culinary network, boasting more than 100 million followers on Facebook and over 1 billion monthly views. That people love food is a gross erosion of the truth.

---

[8] www.webmd.com/diet/news/20200210/how-does-social-media-shape-your-food-choices.

I had to look deeper, and read about how humans are programmed to seek out foods with characteristics that the brain instinctively recognizes as valuable. Calorie-dense food like burgers, biscuits, and white flour treats like pizza typically make people feel good through releasing dopamine and stimulating pleasure centres of the brain. Seeing calorie-dense foods thus leads to anticipating pleasure, so humans focus on food through their eyes. Advertisers and social media content producers know this well.

A famous British study conducted by Lily Hawkins, a doctoral student in Health Psychology at Aston University in Birmingham, revealed that within peer groups, people are more likely to eat what they see their friends on social media indulging in. Participants chose an extra portion of unhealthy snacks and sugary drinks for every three portions they believed their online friends had. This research suggests we may be influenced by our peer group more than we realize when choosing certain foods.[9]

Our species is transforming for sure. Whether it's junk food or a healthier meal, their choices are subconsciously influenced by the pictures they ogle all day long (many of us spend a significant amount of time

---

[9] www.webmd.com/diet/news/20200210/how-does-social-media-shape-your-food-choices.

on one device or another). People are liking, sharing, and commenting on other people's plates.

And that's in addition to the constant pop-up ads for restaurants and fast-food deliveries up through the mechanizations of app developers making money off our smartphones. It is all strategic subliminal marketing that easily ends on our hips, thighs, and sinuses, if we're not careful.

Often, we resort to living vicariously through social media, compensating for our usual family get-togethers and meal times. With limited access to restaurants, coffee shops, and pubs, social media has provided the socially safe distance for recipes and virtual dining.[10] I found that, with the initial lockdowns and uncertainties, many were baking and carb-loading in a very end-of-days attempt to stave off imagined famine. No one knew what was going to happen, right? It made sense as we were propelled into survival mode, staring our mortality in the eye.

Over time, though, I witnessed more healthier eating as people tried to lose the cabin fever, the stress, and the excess weight. Many made new resolutions, revelled in the family time, and experimented with new recipes. Many famous chefs, too, started hosting inspiring

---

[10] https://theconversation.com/foodporn-people-are-more-attracted-to-social-media-content-showcasing-fatty-foods-160221

virtual cooking shows, teaching us how to create nutritious meals with limited ingredients as many suppliers were running short. The social media feeds looked a lot more detox than delectable destruction.

We are constantly bombarded with information, and a click is a move, so we should use these devices to best advantage by sharing informed and researched information—confirm who funded the study and which organizations are involved—rather than simply forwarding random data. Just because you've seen the same message twenty times in one day doesn't make it any more valid or true.

The blessing and the curse of social media is that it can be swift and deadly, helpful and harmful at the same time. Fake news and propaganda sit alongside credible and verifiable information. Some guidelines are not based in science but are fed by politics and economics. It happens with dodgy elections and fly-by-night ministries; and it happens with our food.

The sensationalism inherent in the stories often triggers us emotionally, whether out fear or inspiration and it's too easy to press *Send*. Instead, we could share healthy recipes that have genuinely brought about desired changes or the story of your wellness journey that took off from your garden or kitchen cutting board or the background noise of your juicer. And even then, it might need a disclaimer because our systems are so very different.

THE PANTRY IS FULL BUT WE'RE RUNNING ON EMPTY: THE REAL COST OF A POOR DIET

I'm always inspired by some very true quotes by one of my favourite writers, Michael Pollan:

"Don't buy your food where you buy your gasoline." And finally, "Don't eat anything that won't rot," with the exception of jam and honey, of course. Treats and foods that can survive three years in a tin or packet should allow us to get exercise through raised eyebrows.

He also admonishes us to stay out of the middle of the supermarket, keeping our baskets and trolleys on the straight and narrow of the shop perimeter. Real food tends to be on the outer edges of the store, near the loading docks, where it can be replaced with fresh foods when it goes bad. The middle is a maze of colourful packaging that looks as festive as it is dicey.

Joel Fuhrman MD (2018) uses the term "Fast Food Genocide," because, while many people now realise the dangers of processed food in causing diseases such as obesity, diabetes, heart attacks, strokes, dementia, and cancer, few recognise the strong causative role an unhealthy diet may have in mental illness. A link may even exist between fast food, processed food, commercial baked goods, and sweets, and the destruction of brain cells and a lowering of intelligence.

Sweets and sweetened baked goods stimulate addiction, which can lead to more serious illnesses. Refined carbohydrates may not just lead to being overweight and diabetic but also contribute to dementia, mental illness, and cancer.

He found that people living in urban areas (with relatively high income compared to rural areas), without easy access to whole, fresh foods, live in "food deserts," with reduced availability to nutritious fruits and vegetables.[11] The vulnerable poor in these areas are also at double the risk of heart attack, double the risk of diabetes, and four times the risk of renal failure. Unfortunately, the decrease in life span due to food inequality is shocking but rarely discussed.

Previously, it may have been assumed that high-income households are more at risk due to having more disposable funds for snacks and treats, but new evidence suggests that socio-demographic patterns are changing, and the increasing rate of obesity among the poor has important implications for the distribution of health

---

[11] www.ncbi.nlm.nih.gov/pmc/articles/PMC6146358/.

inequalities. Breadline and low-income populations are equally at risk.[12]

We are faced with the "dual burden" of undernutrition and obesity in countries and communities, but equally in households and even in individuals, who may have excess body fat coexisting with micronutrient deficiencies, such as iron deficiency anaemia, or obesity. Individuals of different generations may also respond differently to social and economic changes, with the younger generation adopting new dietary patterns more quickly, while the elderly continue to eat in more traditional (and sometimes healthier) ways. This is particularly challenging given the relatively low cost and high availability of energy-dense but low-micronutrient-content foods.

Hopefully this brief stock-taking has offered some perspective. Less is more, and we must consciously take control of our nutrition across the food chain, celebrating small and smarter choices.

here are so many fun ways to work around the excuses of not knowing what to cook or not having time. Good food doesn't have to take time to mature like good wine. And it doesn't have to cost all that much, either. Throughout this book I share nuggets and tidbits of

---

[12] www.ncbi.nlm.nih.gov/pmc/articles/PMC3257829/.

science-based and fool-proof recipes that helped me step away from what looked good but wasn't feeding my body, mind ,or spirit.

VITALITY TIPS

➢ You can't remedy what you don't understand: Stay informed. Read, sign up for podcasts, webinars, cooking channels, and nutrition networks (especially the scientific ones!)

➢ Keep food simple, and go for items with few ingredients.

➢ Prioritise healthy recipes as you do every other aspect of your life.

➢ Explore your local market, grocer's, or supermarket like a tourist on a maiden voyage.

➢ Revisit your nutritional and health plan as you co-create a New Normal for you and your family.

CHAPTER THREE

FOOD: A FORCE OF NATURE

Soul and Soil: The Body-Mind-Spirit Connection

While the concept of mind-body-spirit as one interactive entity may seem a bit far out and erudite, here again we should go back to basics.

If you've ever felt "broken" after loss, rejection, or defeat, and were tempted to stay in bed for days, dealing with it, you're familiar with the connection between our soul, thoughts, emotions, and physical body. Or what about the blissful butterflies "love and fresh air" diet, when we are in enchanted all-consuming love? Loss of appetite and energy for days!

When you've felt something "in your gut" intuitively or read that it is actually physiologically possible to die of a broken heart, it may bring you closer to the need for us to think more consciously about what we eat, where we source it from, how much exercise and fulfilment we get from work and relationships, and how we need to understand the interrelationship among our life dimensions.

Centuries ago, people understood this link, but around the seventeenth century, with the body dualism theory of Rene Descartes, came the notion of human beings having separate minds and bodies. This shifted religious theology and medical practice.[13] So much so that, for the longest time, we regarded our brain as our mind and something separate from the rest of our bodies, and the conventional allopathic medical model of treating parts instead of the whole person developed out of this philosophy.

Recent neurological insights now show us that the brain is the critical physical organ influenced by chemistry, biology, electrical currents, and many processes that allow our mind to function. For example, when we experience stress or trauma, our mental processing triggers emotions but also releases survival fight-or-flight chemicals such as adrenaline and cortisol to deal with the situation. In times of perceived danger, our instincts kick in, and we feel bolder, stronger, faster, and uninhibited. Our hearts race, pupils dilate, and the need for sleep and food is virtually zero.

---

[13] www.holistic-mindbody-healing.com/mind-body-spirit-connection.html.

"Stopping for a burger while being chased by a predator," said no one ever. It could help us scale a wall we wouldn't be able to get over otherwise, but prolonged exposure to these chemicals compromises our immunity. Hence, we learn to reframe tough circumstances and manage our triggers through mindfulness and, over time, develop resilience.

It is helpful to understand the mind-body-connection on a cellular level. Cell biologist Bruce Lipton, PhD, equates cells to miniature humans. The cell possesses the same systems and receptors as skin, being aware of its environment and the larger community of cells. The cellular environment is affected by nutrients, poisons, and the perceptions of the individual. In essence, this means our beliefs, attitudes, thoughts, and feelings affect our biology in positive or negative ways.

Cells continually communicate with one another via photons of light in the layer of the human energy field right outside the body. They receive information from the brain and energy field and respond accordingly. When we experience an emotion, our cells experience the same emotion through energy vibrations and changes in body chemistry. Each cell functions independently as well as as a member of the cell groupings that constitute our body.

Science suggests that there are other structures in the human body that function like a brain; our heart would be one such source. The gut, too, is sometimes called a second brain.[14] Research continues to illustrate the phenomenal relationship between overall health and gut bacteria levels; the billions of microbes present in the gut and throughout the body may well exert the greatest influence over us, because they affect how we respond to hunger and how we store fat, and they help us balance glucose levels. More critically, these microbes produce neurotransmitters such as dopamine and serotonin, fundamental to our psychological wellbeing. They influence physiological functioning and communicate directly with the brain.

Clarissa Lenherr, a registered and qualified Nutritional Therapist, believes that looking after gut health, blood sugar levels, and getting enough Vitamin D can greatly improve mental health.[15] In her experience, patients moved from being depressed and anxious to coming off their antidepressants simply by working on their gut health. The use of probiotics was especially important. Probiotics have the good bacteria, which (after a minimum of three weeks) redresses the damage done by antibiotics, bad habits, and general life stress.

---

[14] www.holistic-mindbody-healing.com/mind-body-spirit-connection.html.

[15] Lenherr, Clarissa. "Stressless Strategies for Gut Health." https://clarissalenherr.com.

PSYCHOLOGY AND PHYSIOLOGY

Our thoughts, feelings, beliefs, and attitudes can positively or negatively affect our biology; indeed, our minds can affect how healthy our bodies are. Equally, how we treat our bodies—diet, exercise, sleep—impacts our mental state.[16]

Mental problems can present as physical symptoms; for example, anxiety and overthinking can lead to insomnia and stress. Similarly, physical issues can lead to mental and emotional challenges; consider how an athlete's debilitating injury and persistent pain trigger thoughts of failure, rejection, loss of income, self-confidence, and status, which in turn can lead to isolation and depression. In both these instances, it is likely that remediation might involve therapy, social support, cognitive-behavioural, and even dietary changes. In a world fraught with constant change, fear, busy-ness, and pressure, it's no wonder that stress is an underlying factor in many diseases.

---

[16] www.takingcharge.csh.umn.edu/what-is-the-mind-body-connection.

EFFECTS OF STRESS ON DIGESTION

- ✓ Deregulates our appetite, causing us to overeat or take in little food.

- ✓ Increases cortisol and insulin, which leads to us storing extra body fat, no matter what we eat or how much exercise we get in.

- ✓ Triggers digestive disruption (diarrhea, constipation, irritable bowel symptoms).

- ✓ Loss of nutrients.

- ✓ Destroys healthy gut bacteria.

- ✓ Increases susceptibility to food allergies.

Though this evidence makes clear that there is very little to debate that we are what we eat, and it's a few layers deeper than an apple a day keeping a doctor away, it is helpful to understand that, at a cellular and biochemical level, there is also abundant evidence of the interrelationship between nutrition and mental wellbeing.

The more we nourish our bodies, the more energy and vitality we will enjoy, and our thoughts and emotional lives will be better, too. The addictive chemicals, allergens, and toxic compounds in processed food give us short-term highs, but we are still hungry and have to keep eating. It's highly unlikely that the craving will be for something healthy.

Similarly, when we feel sad, frustrated, or rejected, we're unlikely to sit down calmly and enjoy a healthy salad or soup. Our emotionally supercharged brain is more likely to guide us to refined sugars and dopamine/feel-good ice cream, pizza, and dense carbohydrates. There's scientific truth to the dumped lover dunking their chips into the tub of ice cream while guzzling sugary or alcoholic beverages, as we often see in romantic comedies.

When we don't get enough proper food fuel through nutrients, our brain struggles to do the basics. Even dehydration negatively impacts cognition and processing, so we have to practise self-care throughout the day to keep this wonderfully designed system oiled and maintained.[17]

Whether you're following the eight glasses a day gospel or believe that your water quota is covered by your coffee addiction, the human brain is 75% water and needs water to function optimally. Dehydration is bad for your skin but could also be bad for your mood and your long-term productivity and success. Science tells us that severe dehydration can lead to cognitive problems, including deliriousness and even

---

[17] https://willowcounseling.org/mind-and-body/mind-body-connection-unpacking-the-relationship-between-nutrition-and-mental-health/

unconsciousness, so sip your way to success. Skipping the odd meal because you're engrossed in an exciting project is all right in the short-term, but deficiencies add up, and a lack of nutrients can lead to irritability, poor functioning, and disease over time.

While we may be in the arena of fighting the billion-dollar food companies and using modern technology to find ways to better health, it was the ancient Greeks who introduced civilisation to the concept of energetics and how it affects the fitness of humans, animals, and plants. From the premise that we are all spiritually connected by energy, they practised "wisdom healing," using food to nurture mind, body, and soul.[18]

Perhaps less understood is the fact that different foods have different energies; even two apparently identical vegetables can have a very different impact on your body, if one is 100% organic from rich, fertile soil, grown with love in your backyard, while the other is contaminated with pesticides and harvested with economics-only apathy.

A better life could come from positive thinking, optimism, exercise, and gratitude, but we will also need to invest in highly nutritious foods ethically sourced. Our mindset during meal preparation and enjoyment is

---

[18] https://tropeaka.com/blogs/the-latest/6-nutrition-fundamentals-for-your-mind-body-and-soul.

also important. Healthy food cannot compensate for a restless, panicked, or rushed meal.

Our psychology shapes our physiology; our thoughts and emotions affect our digestion. You need to be in a state where the chemicals and nutrients can be best absorbed into your body. This is why gratitude, awareness, and prayer before any meal are so important. Focus and savour what is on the plate, knowing you are part of something bigger. Picture where it came from, and relish the experience of having something to eat, hopefully with people you love and care for. Name the sensations and emotions coursing through your mind, body, and soul as you nourish yourself.

The mind-body-spirit connection is more than a mere abstraction; it is each of us as a whole being and the beginning of holistic health and thriving. We see the magical interaction when we want to make lasting changes in our lives. Whether you're improving your diet or fitness levels, taking on a new career challenge, or taking your personal relationship to the next level, it will take work at a physical, mental, emotional, and spiritual level.

Anyone who's tried giving up a lifelong addiction through desire or abstinence alone knows it's a little more complicated than that. In later chapters, we consider some key practices for integrating and bringing into equilibrium all the parts of ourselves that help us to enjoy health, vitality, and fulfilment. When we are well, we can give more of ourselves to others on a sustainable basis.

MASTER THE METRICS: KNOW YOUR NUTRIENTS

Essential nutrients are compounds that the human body cannot generate or produce in sufficient quantities. According to the World Health Organization, these nutrients must come from food, where they are best absorbed, and are vital for growth, optimal health, and disease prevention.[19]

There are many essential nutrients, but they can be separated into two categories: namely, macronutrients and micronutrients. Macronutrients are eaten in large amounts and include the primary building blocks of your diet: protein, carbohydrates, and fat. They provide our bodies with energy. Vitamins and minerals are micronutrients, and even small amounts can produce positive health effects. The six main groups of essential micronutrients and macronutrients are thus Proteins, Carbohydrates, Fats, Minerals, Vitamins, and Water.

Variety is the spice of good health, so the goal is to get a balanced mix of foods that naturally are nutrient-

---

[19] www.healthline.com/health/food-nutrition/six-essential-nutrients.

rich. Foods that are nutrient-dense are healthy, as they are low in sugar, sodium, starches, and bad fats.[20] Nutrients are known to reduce our risk for chronic diseases. They are typically found in fruits and vegetables, lean meats, fish, whole grains, dairy, legumes like peas and beans, nuts, and seeds.

Typical of a full pantry leaving us empty, most processed and packaged foods often taste good, but they lack micronutrients while making us pack on empty calories through added sugar, sodium (salt), and saturated or trans fats. From this comes quick release and instant gratification, which leads to long-term challenges like weight gain, obesity, diabetes, and hypertension.

PROTEINS

Protein, in the main, enjoys a good reputation as food sources go. It is vital for good health, providing the building blocks of the body, and not just for muscle. Every cell, from bone to skin to hair, contains protein. A startling 16% of the average human being's body weight is from protein. Protein is used primarily for growth, health, and body maintenance.

---

[20] https://familydoctor.org/changing-your-diet-choosing-nutrient-rich-foods.

All of our hormones, our inner infection fighters called antibodies, and other vital substances are composed of protein. Protein is not used to fuel the body unless it is necessary.

Proteins comprise of different amino acids, and while our bodies can create some amino acids naturally, there are many essential amino acids that can only be sourced through food. We need a variety of amino acids for optimal functioning, and, blessedly, we don't need to eat all of them in one sitting. Our bodies (when healthy) are designed to create complete proteins from the foods we consume throughout the day.

We can get our protein allocation from healthy meat, fish, and egg sources, and also in plant sources like beans, soy, nuts, and some grain variants. The important aspect is to know your numbers. Exactly how much protein you need daily depends on a variety of factors, including age, genetic factors, exercise and activity profile, and so forth. Despite the growing popularity of high-protein diets, there haven't been enough studies to prove that they're healthier or can influence weight loss, according to the Mayo Clinic.[21]

If you enjoy good cutlets of meat, low-fat and lean cuts (without all the over-spicing and sugary marinades)

---

[21]   www.healthline.com/health/food-nutrition/six-essential-nutrients.

offer a good protein source. Baking, broiling, grilling, and roasting are healthy preparation options for meat. Even lean cuts contain more fat and cholesterol compared to other protein sources, so finding an optimal personal health point should guide us, as we find a balanced diet. Chicken breasts (dry or white meat) are a good, higher-protein cut of poultry containing less of the fat contained in the skin or richer brown/dark meat portions, such as the drumstick, wing, or thigh.

Fresh fish and shellfish or frozen or low-salt canned fish are also considered good protein sources. Wild-caught oily fish are the best sources of omega-3 fatty acids and include salmon, tuna, mackerel, and sardines. The idea is for our preparation methods to not destroy nutrients, so poaching, steaming, baking, and broiling are the healthiest ways to prepare fish. Deep-fried fish and too many condiments often spoil and reduce the nutritional value.

Non-meat sources of protein also can be nutrient-rich without the additional high-risk cholesterol impact. A healthy serving of beans, peanut butter, nuts, or seeds can offer this. Include legumes, such as beans, lentils, and chickpeas.

Carbohydrates

Many diets have declared war on carbohydrates, but carbohydrates are necessary for healthy functioning.

They fuel our bodies, especially our central nervous system and brain, and protect us against disease.

For the record and your commitment to good health, know this: *Not all carbs are created equal.* Be slow to judge until you have all the facts. The type of carbohydrate you eat matters and will have different effects on your metabolism. Some carbs are healthier than others. Whole grains, beans, and fibre-rich vegetables and fruits are a way better option than refined grains like chips, biscuits, and products with added sugar.

GRAINS

Whole-grain foods provide high levels of fibre necessary for digestion, as well as maintain satiety; we feel fuller for longer, which could reduce cravings for processed snacks and overeating. Some products contain fibre but are not nutrient-rich, so it is important to check the ingredients list. Rolled or steel-cut oats, brown or wild rice, barley, quinoa, corn on the cob, buckwheat, and wholewheat options are better than the white-flour variants that often contain harmful bleaches and additives and tend to be more addictive or trigger allergic reactions (Chapter 2)

FATS

Fats are certainly one of the sources going through midlife interrogations. They were good then bad, and if the Banterers are anything to go by, they're baiting for good again.

Healthy fats, like good carbs, are an important part of a balanced diet. According to studies conducted by Harvard Medical School, fat supports many physiological functions, such as vitamin and mineral absorption, blood clotting, building cells, and muscle movement. Fats are high in calories, but they offer good energy sources, and the WHO suggests keeping our intake under 30%.

Healthy fats can help balance blood sugar levels, decrease our risks of heart disease and Type 2 diabetes, and improve brain function. Fats are also potent anti-inflammatories, which could decrease the risk of arthritis, cancer, and forms of dementia like Alzheimer's disease.[22]

Unsaturated fats are found in omega-3 and omega-6 fatty acids and provide essential fatty acids we cannot produce on our own. Instead, we can source it from nuts, seeds, fish, and vegetable oil. The goal is to avoid transfats and limit our intake of saturated, animal-based fats like butter, cheese, red meat, and ice cream.

----

[22] www.healthline.com/health/food-nutrition/six-essential-nutrients.

FRUITS AND VEGETABLES

Fruits and vegetables are naturally low in fat. They offer the benefits of nutrients, flavour, colour, inspiration to our culinary creativity, and variety to our diet.

Dark-green vegetables have been known to help us fight off disease and unhealthy weight gain, including broccoli, cauliflower, and Brussels sprouts. Leafy greens such as Swiss chard, spinach, cabbage, romaine lettuce, kale, and bok choy are also great options. There are many vegetables that grow quite easily in our gardens and crop patches that can bring nutritious, wholesome, and versatile options to our table. Squash, carrots, sweet potatoes, turnips, pumpkin, snap peas, green beans, bell peppers, and asparagus can all create delicious snacks, salads, soups, and stews, with or without meat. Even when children are not excited about vegetables, we can camouflage them in soups and even as stir fries or pizza (non-white flour) toppings.

VITAMINS

Vitamins are a word we've probably heard all our lives, starting as early as our toddler days, when we learned that candy and treats were not vitamin vessels. If you know the alphabet, there is a vitamin in there somewhere. There are thirteen essential vitamins that the body needs to function properly, including vitamins A, C, B6, and D.

These powerful micronutrients are vital for warding off disease and maintaining health. Some studies have shown that they may reduce risk of certain types of cancers and boost the immune system. As powerful antioxidants, they effectively prey on and neutralise free radicals, which damage cell membranes and cause a variety of diseases....[23]

So, where do the letters lead us?

Your search for vitamins will take you no farther than your garden, kitchen, or greengrocer's, with fruit and vegetables providing good sources of vitamin C and A and folic acid (a B-group vitamin also important during pregnancy). Grains and cereals are generally good sources of fibre and vitamin B. Full-fat dairy and egg yolks are generally sources of the fat-soluble vitamins A, D, and E. Milk, vegetable oil, or soy bean oil are generally good sources of Vitamin K.[24]

Fruit juices often contain too much sugar and preservatives, but in their purest form, the staple stock is in apples, plums, mangoes, papaya, pineapples, peaches, pears, tomatoes, avocados, grapes, and bananas. Blueberries, strawberries, cherries,

---

[23] www.betterhealth.vic.gov.au/health/healthyliving/ antioxidants#bhc-content.

[24] www1.health.gov.au/internet/publications/publishing.nsf/ Content/canteen-mgr-tr1~nutrients.

pomegranates, and grapes bring colour and a boost to any meal or snack. Homemade juicing and smoothies are great, and adding healthy protein powder or a supplement can take a liquid meal to the next level. Citrus fruits, such as grapefruits and oranges, while offering good fibre, are also renowned for containing vitamin C necessary for fighting colds and flu.

A balanced diet of vegetables and fruit could be sufficient without additional supplements. Vitamin deficiencies can cause problems and disease, and thus we want to include them to improve the health of our eyes, skin, and bones.

MINERALS

Similar to vitamins, minerals help support our bodies, particularly by building strong bones and teeth, regulating your metabolism, and helping us stay sufficiently hydrated. Some of the most common minerals you may have heard or read about include calcium, iron (supports red blood cells and hormone formation), and zinc (immune-system booster and wound repair). Calcium is renowned for fortifying our bones but is also good for maintaining blood pressure levels and muscle functioning.

WATER

Despite what we may tell ourselves when we're addicted to sugar or comfort eating, humans can survive for weeks without food, but we couldn't last even a few days without water.

Often, we reach for something to eat when, in actual fact, we are simply thirsty. (Hence the need for mindful eating, a topic covered in detail in later chapters.) Water is absolutely crucial for every system in your body, and as numbers go, science tells us that approximately 62% of our body weight is water.

It improves our brain function, so we really need it. It acts as a shock absorber and a lubricant. It flushes out toxins, transports nutrients to our cells, keeps us hydrated, and in sufficient quantities can prevent constipation. Whether we're walking, working, or playing in the sun, even mild levels of dehydration can lead to feelings of fatigue and impaired concentration.

The reality is that many of our water sources are seriously lacking and, in some countries, downright toxic. But if you are fortunate enough to have safe water sources, get the good stuff now. Some people are already in the habit of consuming sufficient amounts of water plain, with ice, or even with a slice of orange or lemon.

If you're not one to drink bottles and jugs of water, supplement the few glasses you can manage with fruit and vegetables, which also contain large amounts of water. Celery, cucumber, lettuce, brinjals/eggplants, green cabbage, broccoli, and marrows/courgettes contain more than 80% water. The same applies to fruits such as apricots, oranges, berries, pineapples, plums, and peaches.

The best way to know if you're properly hydrated is the color and volume of your urine. If your urine isn't frequent and pale yellow or nearly clear, you need more water.

Important considerations as you work toward a new whole-health diet includes knowing where you stand in the food journey (it's as personal as your genetic code) and the grocery store (the outer ring is recommended for nutrient-dense foods).

Become conscious about how you can:

* Effortlessly and conveniently add these foods into your daily diet.

* Ensure you have sufficient numbers of nutrients, even as you cut out certain food groups, e.g., going vegetarian, pescatarian (no meat, but eating fish), fruitarian (fruits, nuts, and seeds), or vegan

* Confirm which approved supplements could increase nutrient intake

Note: Most nutrient-rich foods are found in the perimeter of the grocery store. The amount of nutrient-rich foods you should eat depends on your unique daily calorie needs.

Vitamin Deficiencies

One of my favourite verses in the Bible reminds me that we are fearfully and wonderfully made. When I think about how we fit into a broader ecosystem or how our bodies often tell us what we need, we are indeed a work of design perfection. This becomes particularly evident when we think about the delicate balance of nutrients needed for optimal functioning, as well as the conditions that occur when we lack them.

Vitamin deficiencies are especially interesting. They may start off almost negligible, but over time can result in considerable preventable health problems. Let's consider the following scientific findings.

A diet lacking in nutrients potentially causes a variety of unfavourable symptoms that are our body's way of telling us we may need a top-up or rebalance our vitamins and minerals. The self-management secret is that we stay informed, so we recognize these deficiencies as early as possible. Most often, a change in diet can easily help us to recalibrate.

Throughout this section, I stress again the importance of personalised assessment and monitoring. There are often more than one triggers or sources for a particular condition. The good news, of course, is that vitamin deficiencies are easily redressed through basic nutrition. Supplements should be administered only on the professional word of a healthcare professional.

Common symptoms of vitamin deficiency:

* *Brittle hair and nails*

Several factors could lead to brittle hair and nails, but one of them is a lack of biotin or vitamin B7, a nutrient needed to help our bodies convert food into energy. A deficiency in biotin is very rare but could present as brittle, thinning, or splitting hair and nails. It also presents as chronic fatigue, muscle pain, cramps, and tingling in the hands and feet.[25]

Pregnancy, digestive disorders, excessive smoking, and alcohol abuse all increase the risk of a vitamin B7 deficiency. As with many other deficiencies, prolonged use of medications such as antibiotics also increases risk. Foods that are rich in biotin include egg yolks, organ meats, fish, meat, dairy, nuts, seeds, spinach, broccoli, cauliflower, sweet potatoes, yeast, whole grains, and bananas

* *Lesions in and around the mouth*

Lesions, ulcers and cracks in and around the mouth may, to some degree, be linked to a lack of iron or B vitamins. A significant number of patients with mouth

---

[25] www.healthline.com/nutrition/vitamin-deficiency

ulcers show deficiencies in thiamine (vitamin B1), riboflavin (vitamin B2), and pyridoxine (vitamin B6).

Another condition known as angular cheilitis, which causes the corners of the mouth to crack, split, or bleed, can cause dehydration but has also been linked to deficiencies. This can easily be remedied by eating more foods rich in iron, including poultry, meat, fish, legumes, dark leafy greens, nuts, seeds, and whole grains.

★ *Bleeding gums*

Bleeding gums and even tooth loss, if not due to mechanical failure such as a rushed toothbrushing job, could also be symptomatic of a vitamin C deficiency. This vitamin, well known for helping with overcoming colds, plays a vital part in wound repair, increased immunity, and as an antioxidant prevents cell damage. Another serious result of severe vitamin C deficiency is scurvy, a condition that depresses the immune system, weakens bones and muscles, and leads to fatigue and lethargy. Other commonplace indicators include a propensity to bruise easily, slower healing, frequent nosebleeds, and very dry skin.

Despite our many superpowers, our bodies cannot produce vitamin C on their own. That means we have to consume it through a diet and fresh fruits and vegetables; this is the simplest way to get our daily quota.

★ *Vision impacts*

If you're still wondering about carrots and eyesight, it is well researched that a diet poor in vitamins can cause vision problems. Diets with insufficient amounts of vitamin A have been linked to night blindness, which reduces the ability to see in low light or in darkness. This happens because vitamin A is needed for the production of rhodopsin, a pigment found in the retina that helps us see at night. Left untreated, night blindness can develop into xerophthalmia, a condition that damages the cornea and can culminate in complete blindness.

Vitamin A deficiency presents more in developing countries and could be redressed through consuming more vitamin-A-rich foods, such as organ meats, dairy, eggs, fish, dark leafy greens, and yellow-orange-coloured vegetables.

As with much of life, balance is critical. It becomes very tempting to consume vitamins, as pharmaceutical companies and retail pharmacies advertise healthcare products with as much excitement as others would the latest gadget or automobile. Medications and supplements are marketed as the elixirs of longevity and wellbeing. But it is important to take supplements only when a severe deficiency is diagnosed. An excess of vitamin A could easily lead to toxicity. Symptoms of vitamin A toxicity can be serious and include nausea, headaches, skin irritation, joint and bone pain, and, in severe cases, even coma or death.[26]

★ *Dry, scaly patches and dandruff*

Certain dermatological conditions and dandruff are skin disorders that affect parts of your body that naturally produce necessary oils and present as itchy, flaking skin. They could be the result of several factors, but a nutrient-poor diet can also be a culprit.

Low blood levels of zinc, niacin (vitamin B3), riboflavin (vitamin B2), and pyridoxine (vitamin B6) may each play a role. Foods rich in these vitamins include whole grains, poultry, meat, fish, eggs, dairy, organ meats, legumes, green vegetables, starchy vegetables, nuts, and seeds. Seafood, meat, legumes, dairy, nuts, and wholegrains are all great sources of zinc.

★ *Hair loss*

Hair loss is a very common symptom, and nutrients like iron, zinc, vitamins B3 and B7, linoleic acid (LA), and alpha-linolenic acid (ALA) potentially prevent or slow down hair loss. Forget the expensive shampoos and leave-in chemical products for healthy hair. Instead,

---

[26] www.healthline.com/nutrition/vitamin-deficiency.

stock up on your nutritional conditioners, such as free-range meat, fish, dairy, whole grains, legumes, nuts, seeds, and leafy greens. Leafy vegetables, nuts, whole grains, and vegetable oils are rich in LA, while walnuts, flax seeds, chia seeds, and soy nuts are rich in ALA.

VITAMIN D DEFICIENCY

Vitamin D strengthens bones (through improving calcium absorption) and may help prevent some cancers; a deficiency can include muscle weakness, pain, fatigue and even fractures as a result of weak bones.

We can prevent many serious conditions such as cardiovascular disease, hypertension, diabetes, infections, some types of cancer, and even multiple sclerosis with sufficient amounts of vitamin D.

Vitamin D is distinctive because our skin can produce it by using sunlight. This is a good thing, because it doesn't occur naturally in food like many other vitamins do. It is added to some foodstuffs and should appear on the ingredients list.

Food and sunlight are the best natural sources of vitamin D. Of course, with our ozone challenges, too much direct sunlight for prolonged periods of time poses increased risks of skin cancer, but a few minutes every week is enough. It appears that fairer skin and youth render this process easier than for those over fifty and the darker-skinned.[27]

A deficiency is easily detected through a blood test. Food sources rich in vitamin D include cheese, liver, beef, sardines, cod liver oil, tuna, orange juice, milk and yoghurt, and certain cereals.

HORMONAL BALANCE AND DIET

Hormones are the chemical messengers of the endocrine system that support growth and development, metabolism and digestion, fertility, stress, mood, and many fundamental physiological processes. We have more than 200 hormones in our bodies. Estrogen, testosterone, cortisol, insulin, leptin, ghrelin, and thyroid hormones are the most commonly known. These are linked closely to metabolism, fertility, and mood.

Eating a diet high in fruits, vegetables, whole grains, healthy fats, and protein contributes to hormonal balance. Insufficient calories, healthy fats, or fibre can deregulate hormones and may lead to conditions like obesity, diabetes, infertility, and cancer. Lack of sleep, stress, alcohol, and eating processed foods can also throw off hormones, directly or indirectly, by

---

[27] https://my.clevelandclinic.org/health/articles/15050-vitamin-d--vitamin-d-deficiency.

influencing the gut microbiome, which keeps hormones balanced.[28]

When hormones become imbalanced, as a result of too much or too little being produced or something interfering with signalling pathways, it results in dysfunction. And this is not limited to menopause; it happens to men and women throughout our lives. What we eat affects the production of hormones and their signalling pathways.

Melissa Groves Azzaro, RDN, LD, PCOS, hormone and fertility dietitian, recommends eating good healthy fats, like olive oil, avocado, nuts, and seeds; fibre sources like fruits and vegetables; and quality proteins like eggs, fish, and meat. We should avoid pesticides, alcohol, and artificial sweeteners, which have been shown to negatively impact hormones. Artificial sweeteners in particular may alter gut bacteria, which may impact the balance of hunger and satiety; the hormones that tell us when we are hungry and full become out of sync.[29]

Foods that are most helpful during perimenopause and menopause are omega-3-rich foods, such as oily fish, chia seed, and flax seeds. A study published in *The*

---

[28] www.eatingwell.com/article/7805452/hormone-balancing-foods-how-diet-can-help/.

[29] www.eatingwell.com/article/7805452/hormone-balancing-foods-how-diet-can-help/.

American Journal of Clinical Nutrition showed that a diet rich in omega 3s helped to reduce the frequency of hot flashes in menopausal women.[30]

In addition to a healthy diet, hormonal balance also requires adequate sleep and exercise and proactive stress management. Keeping stress levels low and exercising regularly are all crucial for hormone balance. Sleep deprivation is linked to low testosterone in men, and lack of sleep interferes with leptin and ghrelin, our hunger and satiety hormones. This explains why we want bad carbs and treats when we're tired or irritated.

Chronic stress triggers elevated levels of a survival hormone called cortisol, which in turn suppresses the digestive and immune systems and can precipitate high blood pressure. Cortisol also leads to carbohydrate cravings. Exercise, prayer, meditation, and rest boost levels of norepinephrine (uplifting energy) and serotonin (feel-good hormone).

Your remedies are in your garden. When I turned forty, my hormonal clock started ticking. I panicked, as I didn't want to feel odd or old, so I resorted to supplements such as magnesium, B vitamins, probiotics, omega-3 fatty acids, vitamin D3, and many more, just so I could regulate my hormonal activity. Suffice it to say

---

[30] https://ourworld.unu.edu/en/how-things-work-ecological-food-systems.

they were slightly helpful, but my biggest revelation came from food.

I can say this with utmost confidence: your hormonal imbalance remedies are all in your diet. My menu soon included a mixture of avocados, leafy vegetables, cashews, tuna fish, flax seeds, pumpkin seeds, dark chocolate (this I can't stress enough), legumes, tofu, whole grains, fatty fish, bananas, soy beans, almonds, sesame seeds, and cruciferous vegetables, with herbs and spices in abundance. With these foods, I have been able to balance my hormones.

PREBIOTICS AND PROBIOTICS

Probiotics are the good bacteria that reside in the gut, while prebiotics are specialized plant fibres eaten by those bacteria.

The gut is the largest endocrine organ in the body, synthesizing and secreting more than twenty hormones that are key to our appetite, satiety, and metabolism. Prebiotic foods, like raw garlic and oats, asparagus, dandelion, almonds, apples, and bananas, are helpful, as are probiotics found in yoghurt.

ANTI-AGEING AND DIET

Looking at the content of our adverts, one of our greatest obsessions has to be staving off the signs of ageing. It reminds us of our mortality, and in a society fixated on (often superficial) appearance and success, brands are often built on looks and first impressions.

Very few of us appreciate the stories and memories and grace behind scars, laugh lines, and wrinkles; most of us watch with trepidation the black and brown hairs turn to grey. Dentistry, bariatric, and cosmetic surgery have become trillion-dollar industries, and there are plastic surgeons who make a living out of fixing the mistakes of other plastic surgeons, with devastating results. Our devices have applications that encourage us to look perfect and flawless, whatever that means, while filters and Photoshop have taken us into an augmented reality.

But despite all of that, everything has a season, and the question is not that we will age and die, but rather that we enjoy good health for as long as possible. Diet is a good place to start for providing anti-ageing (or graceful ageing) options.

Naturally, genetics plays a vital role in our appearance and how we age, but so does healthy living. We cannot stop the ageing process, but it is now a well-known fact that the foods we eat and what we drink play a significant role in how well we age.

It's a maintenance, vitality, and sustainability game rather than merely focusing on aesthetics. You're going to have to work for your health, through good food and activity choices, and the earlier the better. Hard manual labour and too many hours in the sun can negatively impact our posture and skin, for example. But there are natural ways to improve our wellbeing. The right nutritional choices along with a healthy lifestyle can keep you youthful at any age. Looking around my social and professional circles, the individuals getting the most joy and fulfilment are healthy, confident, and attractive at any age as they work toward holistic wellness—body, mind, and soul.

As we age, our skin may become more dry, while weight maintenance and muscle density need extra attention and some effort. Health and wellness come from diet and lifestyle, and both might need adjustment. Exercise, enough sleep, good nutrients and antioxidants, good stress management, and letting go of toxic relationships can all bring us toward longevity.

The goal is to fight off inflammation and infection. Timothy Harlan, MD, an assistant professor of medicine at Tulane University School of Medicine, states that "aging is basically a chronic inflammatory state."[31] Here, diet becomes important when we understand that some foods cause inflammation while others negate it.

Consuming too much sugar and processed carbohydrates (like pasta, bread, and baked goods) in

---

[31] www.webmd.com/diet/features/is-your-diet-aging-you#1.

time damages your skin's collagen, which is needed for keeping skin springy and wrinkle resistant, according to Andrea Giancoli, MPH, RD. Pro-inflammatory foods promote wrinkles and accelerate ageing and storage of body fat. These include refined sugar, artificial sweeteners, processed cereals, processed meats, white flour, and trans fats. Instead, choose food as close to its natural form as possible, because it can cure and nourish. Natural condiments and enhancers like ginger and turmeric are so versatile and have been known to reduce joint pain from inflammatory conditions like arthritis.

According to a study published in the *Asia Pacific Journal of Clinical Nutrition*, your next curry could be the way to staying fabulous and fit, because turmeric and cumin have shown potential to prevent DNA damage and help DNA repair.[32] It could even be simpler with anti-ageing beverages, like green tea or a berry smoothie, or a natural salad dressing with extra virgin olive oil. That's juicy news, if you're into preventing disease and slowing down the ageing process.

Often, the anti-ageing fight starts too late, when there's too much damage already from excessive smoking and alcohol abuse, long nights, juggling jobs

---

[32] https://thehealthychef.com/blogs/wellbeing/your-anti-ageing-nutrition-plan.

and priorities, and burning boxes of candles on both ends. Ideally, we should start healthy eating in our childhood and youth. Our teens, twenties, and thirties are often the roughest, as we spread ourselves thin, getting everything done and being all over the place for our careers and our families, while navigating social FOMO (Fear of Missing Out). Soon enough, we're too exhausted for the all-nighters, and recovery takes many days longer. But it's never too late to make the necessary changes.

Protein helps to maintain lean muscle, support a healthy weight, and nourish firmer, healthier skin.

Sleep helps with general immunity and stress reduction. There are a plethora of studies relating sleep deprivation to unfavourable and unstable emotional responses and weight gain. It's also great for the skin, so while you're figuring out the next big thing, take yourself off to bed for a nap.

Water is also one of the best sources of keeping our skin looking and feeling young and vibrant. Our skin, as the largest organ, is often the canvas that tells us what is going on inside, for better or worse. Many cosmetic serums, lotions, masks, and creams promise timeless youth and magical coverage, but nothing beats good old-fashioned rejuvenating water. Whether we're bathing or drinking sufficient quantities each day, we'll feel renewed inside and out.

Pomegranates have been used for centuries as a healing medicinal fruit. High in vitamin C and a variety of potent antioxidants, pomegranates may protect us from free-radical damage and reduce inflammation levels. They contain the compound punicalagins, which helps to preserve collagen in the skin, slowing signs of ageing.

The antioxidant profile of *dark chocolate* is even more powerful than acai berries, blueberries, and cranberries. Chocolate contains antioxidants called flavanols, which protect the skin from sun damage. Studies reveal that people consuming high-flavanol variants experienced improved blood flow to the skin and improvements in thickness, hydration, and smoothness. The goal is to choose at least 70% cocoa solids, because the higher the number, the greater flavanol content.[33]

Bone broth is also a great option. Combining chicken bones with water and veggie scraps makes a cheap and healthy alternative. The longer you allow it to simmer, the more collagen and gelatin are released from the bones, which gives the broth a thicker texture. It might not appear terribly attractive, but *you* will, because it is

---

[33] Groth, Leah. *30 Anti-Aging Foods for Beautiful Skin.* https://lauracipullo.com/wp-content/uploads/2020/02/30-Anti-aging-Foods-for-Beautiful-Skin-October-2018.pdf.

filled with collagen, amino acids, and minerals that promote healthy, younger looking skin.

Red bell peppers are loaded with antioxidants and are awesome anti-ageing agents. In addition to their high content of vitamin C—great for collagen production—they contain powerful antioxidants called carotenoids (the plant pigments responsible for the bright-red, yellow, and orange colours in many fruits and vegetables). They have a variety of anti-inflammatory properties and may help protect skin from sun damage, pollution, and environmental toxins.

There are many other sources of nutritional anti-age supporters that will be introduced as I share some of my favourite go-to recipes, but it is clear that your Pretty from the Plate remedies are within reach.

Go for Glow with nature's nurses and beauticians: blueberries, dark chocolate, broccoli, salmon, avocado, spinach, nuts, pomegranate, figs, papaya (improves skin elasticity), and red bell peppers. Papayas contain an enzyme called papain, which provides anti-ageing benefits by working as one of nature's best anti-inflammatories. It's also found in many exfoliating products, so you can chew your way to great looks while saving your gut from the harmful effects of anti-inflammatories. They're under your nose and no further than your garden.

Get back to nature. That is where all your answers lie for combating muscle fatigue, neutralizing free radicals, reducing DNA damage, and naturally detoxifying. Your mind, body, spirit, and mirror will be glad you did.

THE IMPORTANCE OF A HEALTHY ECOSYSTEM

When I understood the mind-body-soul system better, it became clear that it's not just what we eat, but it is about energy and where it comes from.

How and where foods are planted, cultivated, and harvested matter. How animals are raised and culled for food matter, because that energy combines with our energy, impacting our life processes on various levels. The other aspect pertains to the manufacturing and often the mass-production infrastructure that pushes profits above health and sustainability. There are natural environments in danger of extinction because of greed and short-term perspectives.

I came to see that food production, consumption, and health are also about economics and politics. A massive realignment is needed, because there is an accelerated and cumulative misalignment between human biology and modern industrial society. Many food production practices intended to provide sources of nourishment are instead responsible for an increase in deaths due to non-communicable chronic diseases such as obesity, diabetes, cardiovascular diseases, and cancer. Industrial-level agriculture produces inexpensive, low-nutrient food in excessive quantities. Extensive use of antibiotics in livestock farming and agricultural pesticides and fertilizers intensify the risk of groundwater contamination as massive amounts of animal waste and run-off laden degrade our soil, water and air.[34]

Approximately 40% of the world's agricultural land is now seriously degraded. UN figures indicate that an area of fertile soil the size of Ukraine is lost every year because of poor farming practices. And it's happening everywhere. In essence, a new system of agriculture is needed to prevent mass starvation, because, to get back to basics: No soil = no food.[35]

The survival of our species will also rely on many more non-toxic, infinitely recyclable and biodegradable products. Many experts believe we need to rethink our agricultural strategies and practices, viewing farms as the ecosystems that they are. When they are not designed with this self-sustaining infrastructure in mind, they usually require many outside inputs, including fossil fuels and organic matter that are

---

[34] https://foodprint.org/issues/how-our-food-system-affects-public-health/.
[35] https://ourworld.unu.edu/en/how-things-work-ecological-food-systems.

fundamentally unsustainable, and some are harmful to production.

The ability to produce an excess of food cheaply comes from monocropping. This describes the cultivation of a single crop on the same piece of land repeatedly over successive seasons, without crop rotation. Whereas natural and sustainable farming practices control weeds, insects, and other pests with ecosystem management, farmers who monocrop are dependent on pesticides. These fertilizers add back nitrogen, phosphorus, and potassium into the depleted land—soil that would otherwise naturally revive itself by crop rotation (or via animal manure or compost) in a sustainable farming system. At certain amounts and/or exposure levels, certain pesticides, herbicides, and fertilizers are harmful to humans and the surrounding environment.[36]

THE CASE FOR HOMEGROWN FARE

The modern food system relies on large-scale crop production practices that produce food grown specifically for high yields, ease of transport, and fast growth. This infrastructure has resulted in a proliferation of inexpensive, nutritionally poor foods made predominantly from crops such as corn, wheat,

---

[36] https://foodprint.org/issues/how-our-food-system-affects-public-health/.

and soybeans, resulting in a lack of nutritional diversity in broad-based diet. These very crops are also used to bulk up animals in the shortest possible time and have replaced healthier, grass-fed animal protein sources.

Added to this, many governments support these farmers financially, the result being low-quality, unsustainable meat brought to our supermarket shelves. Through eating this meat, we eat grains, whether we want to or not, often with harmful allergic side effects.

The nutrient content of animal products has also declined with the rise of industrialized meat production. Larger mechanised dairies produce higher yields of milk, but it effectively contains lower concentrations of protein, fat, and milk components. Beef produced in these facilities often contains lower levels of important nutrients and are higher in LDL (the "bad") cholesterol.

On the other hand, research indicates that grass-fed cows produce meat and milk with higher levels of omega-3 fatty acids, high-quality fats, and precursors for vitamins A and E. Grass-fed, organic dairy provides a balance of fatty acids at a ratio close to one for omega-6 and omega-3, which is thought to be more ideal for health. Likewise, eggs from pastured hens are also found to contain less unhealthy omega-6 fatty acids and more omega-3 fatty acids, as well as more Vitamin E.

Food safety also becomes an issue as foodborne illness is, for the most part, underreported but precipitates dangers along the food supply chain. Contamination can occur at the farm, during processing and distribution, as well as further down, at points of sale and service or eventually as we cook at home. And no one would be the wiser.

This risk increases with industrialised production. For instance, a crop sprayed with contaminated water could infect thousands of consumers. If contaminated meat makes it to the supermarket shelves, it would be hard to trace back to farm operations. Animal slaughter and processing facilities are particularly prone to the spread of harmful bacteria; for that reason, I believe healthcare protocols must be strictly observed. Increased rates of production can make it hard for workers to take the necessary care to prevent contamination nevertheless.

The message became so clear for me: Planting and rearing our own food resources are the best ways to preserve the environment whilst controlling what makes it to our plates. Vegetable and herb gardens, water purification plants, and food forests range in size and shape and can be developed in rural and urban areas. You could have a healthy plot of land, garden patch, or window ledge herb garden. Replenish your crops with seeds, leftovers, and make your own fertilizer and mulch.

I'm always encouraged to see how schools and even corporate offices incorporate recycling bins into their day-to-day operations. Doing the same at home becomes a way of life for the family and is great for the garden, too, which is in essence our food and our medicine.

With a move toward more ethical consumerism, people are becoming more knowledgeable about where their food comes from. Industrial agriculture causes environmental impacts as well as health problems associated with obesity and other lifestyle diseases in affluent nations and hunger in poorer countries. Thus, we are consciously and intentionally strategizing toward healthy, sustainable eating.

Cultivating your own produce also circumvents the problems of rising prices. Years ago, fruit and vegetables were among the cheapest products you could buy. These days, due to agricultural problems and climate change impacts, it's harder and more expensive to grow certain types of produce. Some higher-end stores sell imported fruit and vegetables coming from far-off lands and spending a fair amount of time in refrigeration chambers. So, they look great and shiny in the air-conditioned supermarkets but go brown and rot very quickly in your vegetable basket at home. Many also taste more artificially sweetened, and some are just watery and tasteless.

GRASSROOTS: THE POWER OF A PLANT-BASED DIET

There is no specific definition or plan for plant-based eating. Some people consider plant-based eating to be following a vegetarian or vegan lifestyle that eliminates most or all animal products. Others consider it aiming to eat more plant-based foods while decreasing, but not eliminating, animal products.

> *Plant-based eating is a more nutritional strategy than a "diet." A simple way to look at it is that at least 60-75% of your foods come from plants such as vegetables, fruits, beans, grains, nuts, and seeds.*[37]

According to dietitian Sue Radd, following a plant-based diet concentrated on fruits, vegetables, whole grains, and legumes, potentially retards or prevents various processes of disease that begin long before diagnosis. It is helpful to think that some diseases develop over time and as such could be prevented or treated proactively.

For the most part, this brings us to dietary choices as the foundation of holistic improvement. Many countries are seeing an increase in plant-based eating through

---

[37] https://pearlpoint.org. "The Power of Plant-Based Eating."

greater awareness of the health and environmental benefits that come along with it.

Plant-based foods contain a complex mix of beneficial chemicals and fibre sources that work together to lower oxidative stress, stifle inflammation, target your microbiome, and lower insulin resistance.[38] These beneficial phytochemicals, vitamins, minerals, and fibres are hard to consume in sufficient amounts through the typical Western diet of fifty percent animal protein.

Plant-based foods are often lower in calories than animal products. Foods containing these curative compounds are often brightly coloured or strong in flavour, and they are much better (and cheaper) than the supplements lining the shelves in stores and pharmacies.

The diet's efficacy is seen through combinations of natural plant-based food eaten regularly. If you're a die-hard carnivore, the good news is that adopting a plant-based diet doesn't mean becoming vegan or vegetarian. Instead, it involves consuming a variety of vegetables, legumes, unrefined grains, nuts and seeds, and whole fruits.

---

[38] www.abc.net.au.

In previous sections, we saw how cancer prevention is another aspect in which diet has been found to have significant impact. Around sixty percent of cancers are associated with diet and lifestyle. According to the American Institute for Cancer Research, phytochemicals (phytonutrients) are a powerful cancer-fighting component able to:

➤ Ward off cancer-cell formation and replication

➤ Rebuild healthy cells including those needed for immunity

➤ Regulate hormones

➤ Reduce certain kinds of inflammation[39]

According to nutritionist Lauren Manaker, RDN, research reveals many heart-health benefits linked to plant-forward diets, including reduced cholesterol. Other studies suggest it may improve fertility parameters, as well as reduce the risk of developing Type 2 diabetes. A review published in the July 2018 *Frontiers in Public Health* journal supports this perspective.[40]

A scientific review published in October 2018 in *BMJ Open Diabetes Research & Care* illustrated how following a

---

[39] www.abc.net.au. "Eating for better health: The power of plant-based diets."

[40] www.everydayhealth.com/diet-nutrition/plant-based-diet-food-list-meal-plan-benefits-more/.

plant-based diet can positively impact the emotional and physical wellbeing, quality of life, and general health of those living with Type 2 diabetes, while also improving their physical markers.

There are also numerous studies suggesting that diets containing higher levels of plant protein are linked to lower rates of early death from all causes; and a study published in July 2020 in the *BMJ* found that participants whose diets contained the most plant-based protein had a six-percent lower risk of premature death than individuals who consumed less protein overall.[41] Three to four servings per day of fruits, vegetables, and legumes can result in lower risk of all-causes of early deaths.

Doubling your portion of vegetables, trying a new fruit each week, including vegetables with your lunch, and adding extra vegetables to all recipes are great steps. There are a huge variety of plant-based foods you can incorporate into your diet, but learning how to cook them is essential.

PLANT-FORWARD EATING PATTERNS

If you're curious or suffering from tastebud fatigue from months and years of unhealthy eating, a plant-based strategy may be a welcome change. It can be a gradual

---

[41] www.everydayhealth.com/diet-nutrition/plant-based-diet-food-list-meal-plan-benefits-more/.

addition of fruits, vegetables, whole grains, and legumes.

Most plans suggest 25% animal protein and 75% plant-based foods. If you're going for the highest nutrient content, opt for colourful vegetables and fruits. Some days, you may want to go full-on plant-based or replace up to two meals with beans, nuts, seeds, or slow-release breads like pumpkin or potato bread.

A delicious bean curry with lots of fresh coriander and some great pumpkin flour bread can be just as filling as a meat curry with rice, roti, or naan. And of course, it will take less time. Winner!

VEGETARIAN VARIATIONS

Vegetarian diets come in many shapes and sizes, and you can choose the version that best suits your health and lifestyle needs. They demonstrate positive impacts to support health, including a lower risk of developing coronary heart disease, high blood pressure, or diabetes, and increasing longevity.

Semi-vegetarian or flexitarian: eggs, dairy, occasional meat, fillet, fish and seafood

Pescatarian: eggs, dairy, fish, seafood, NO meat or poultry

Vegetarian: eggs, dairy, NO meat, poultry, fish or other seafood

Vegan: NO animal food in any form[42]

Chapter Two alerted us to the many landmines of processed and pre-packaged foods, and how toxic additives make their way into even the healthiest-looking alternatives. Be sure to choose less-processed plant-based foods with fewer ingredients. The longer the list, the smaller the fine print, the harder to read, and the tougher to digest.

Be conscious and kind to yourself as you make these shifts. Our mind-body-soul composition is unique, and what works like a charm for one person could catapult another onto a battlefield of allergies and sensitivities. If your gut isn't excited about bread or pasta, no matter how delicious it looks, it isn't worth the suffering of cramps, bloating, and reflux hours later after a thirty-minute meal. There are gentler (and equally delicious) alternatives that will leave you feeling energised and sufficiently fuelled to take on the next task.

You will eventually find your perfect mix. Perhaps you enjoy a crispy salad with homemade dressing. Or it may turn out that steamed vegetables with some herbs

---

[42] www.health.harvard.edu/blog/what-is-a-plant-based-diet-and-why-should-you-try-it-2018092614760#:~:text=Plant%2D based% 20or%20plant%2Dforwardnever%20eat%20meat%20 or%20dairy.

bring on the feel-good of family times and Sunday lunch vibes in half the time.

As a working mom, I need the goodness and the gap. Time, energy, and quality are non-negotiables for me, so experimenting in the kitchen is both pleasure and passion. There's no tolerance for wastage, and while fruits and vegetables tend to go off faster during warmer seasons, they can be added to soups or smoothies or made into icy treats and frozen.

I enjoy good free-range meat, but it doesn't have to be the main event on my plate. I know the "fries and a shake" accompaniment to steaks and burgers has become popular with restaurants and food franchises, but sometimes a smaller portion of ethically sourced meat is my accompaniment to green goodness. Good fats from avocados, nuts, nut butters like almond butter, and olive oil bring lower-risk flavour and satiety.

Through my journey of becoming more conscious about food, I've learned to listen to what I need rather than reflexively reach for what I *think* I need. Some days, I want baked cheesecake, and some days, I want barley. Sometimes, all I need is juicy apples, apricots, or cooling slices of watermelon instead of complicated meals and desserts.

FOOD INVESTIGATOR MEETS CHEF

With all the knowledge available about nutrients, food groups, the importance of variety, and the intelligence around food labels and sources, the next step is creating soul food.

Dr. Stanton calls it "food literacy," which means "being aware of where your food comes from, how it's grown and distributed, and how to prepare it in ways that don't destroy its nutritional value ... Becoming familiar with and confident in cooking ingredients you might not have used before is a part of the process."[43] The good news is you can do it right in your kitchen, and you won't need state-of-the-art appliances and gadgets either.

Stir fry, braising, and grilling often mean less oil, more retained texture, nutrients, and flavour, and virtually only minutes of preparation time.

---

[43] https://www.abc.net.au Eating for better health The power of plant based diets

VITALITY TIPS

- ➤ *Eat to feed mind, body, and soul.*

- ➤ *Thriving is about getting back to basics and understanding yourself at a cellular level all the way through to holistic health.*

- ➤ *Keep a Food Journal, and make the connections between what and when you eat, how you prepare it, and how it makes you feel.*

- ➤ *Investigate viable ways of producing natural and healthy foods at home.*

- ➤ *Cook your way to good health, and stave off the ravages of time with natural food and drink.*

- ➤ *Manage stress and tension, and become unapologetic about what and who fills your cup (and your plate).*

CHAPTER FOUR

OUR RELATIONSHIP STATUS WITH FOOD: COMPLICATED

Lifestyle Diseases and Food

One of our greatest developmental paradoxes is that we're finding the methods, medications, and means to live longer, but we're not living healthier lifestyles. Perhaps, as we pursue more money, status, things, and accomplishments, *more* is making it all the more complicated. We're running and rushing and taking shortcuts and arguably not standing still long enough to smell the roses and reevaluate.

Sadly, this unconscious living will impact our children and adolescents as well, and in countries like Australia and the US, incidents of children diagnosed with life-threatening Type 2 diabetes is on the rise. A young person diagnosed with diabetes is likely to die fifteen years earlier than other children their age.[44]

Now that our youngsters are digital natives, they spend more time indoors, sitting or lying down, enjoying their electronic devices, rather than running about until sunset like we did in our youth. In many crime-infested areas, children are cooped up inside, studying, watching television, or surfing the Internet. Activity is fast on the decline, and takeaways delivered to the doorstep are on the rise. Every day, we are bombarded with high-life adverts promoting the consumption of foods containing high levels of sugar, salt, refined carbohydrates, saturated fat, and cholesterol. Fast food and a faster downward spiral to death. But all is not lost.

I am inspired by *National Geographic* researcher Dan Buettner's lessons from five communities around the world whose citizens do not die early due to chronic diseases. In these "Blue Zones" (California, Costa Rica, Italy, Greece and Japan), their inhabitants generally live well into their nineties and beyond without the physical, financial, and emotional costs associated with disability

[44] www.sanitarium.com.au/health-nutrition/nutrition/foods-that-fight-lifestyle-diseases.

or disease. They share common lifestyle factors that boost longevity and quality of life.

In the main, they regard food as medicine, not just hunger busters. Most stay physically active well into their last years, avoiding processed foods, growing their own foods, and consuming very little meat, if at all. If they sound like the "Others" in a sci-fi movie, all this really proves is that they have used their free will to choose a more meaningful, purposeful life, and they want to stay well enough to enjoy each day fully. They pursue meaning and a reason to get up each day, not offended by an alarm clock or the prospect of a job they despise or reaching for a mobile phone or To Do list of survival things before they have expressed gratitude for another day. They see the bigger picture, giving back to their communities, teaching the young, maintaining healthy connections, and immersing themselves in jobs and relationships that are fulfilling rather than draining.

DEFINING LIFESTYLE DISEASES

Lifestyle diseases are ailments resulting from daily habits that limit activity and instead urge towards a more sedentary routine. They cause several health issues that potentially precipitate chronic non-communicable diseases with near life-threatening consequences.

Genetics, physiology, environment, and behaviours are all predisposing factors to non-communicable lifestyle diseases. Behavioural factors include consumption of tobacco, metabolic disorders from an unhealthy diet, insufficient physical activity, and alcohol abuse. Elevated blood pressure, increased blood glucose (hyperglycaemia), raised blood lipids (increased levels of fat in the blood), and obesity are consequences of this risky lifestyle. These risks are modifiable, and so, with better choices, we can overhaul our daily routines.

According to the World Health Organization, more than 7 million people die each year from tobacco consumption, and the fatality rate is projected to increase markedly. Excessive sodium intake causes more than four million deaths annually, while alcohol abuse causes 1.65 million deaths. Basic lack of physical activity claims around 1.6 million lives annually. One can only imagine that, during the COVID lockdowns, these problems were exacerbated.

FOODS THAT COMBAT AND REVERSE LIFESTYLE DISEASES

Buettner's Blue Zone findings have been backed up by science, particularly studies conducted by the World Cancer Research Fund and the American Institute of Cancer Research, which highlight lower rates of cancer, hypertension, and diabetes in plant-based diets high in fibre. The following are highly recommended options for bringing vitality: wholewheat breads, cereals, broccoli, green leafy vegetables, apples, tomatoes, onions, garlic, berries, avocado, red grapes, nuts, seeds, legumes, herbs and spices (e.g., turmeric), soy beans, soy milk, and tofu.

The good news is that effecting even small, gradual changes to our diet and lifestyle kickstarts the journey toward wholeness. By changing what and how we eat, we can prevent up to seventy percent of chronic disease and premature death. Similarly, basic lifestyle and activity changes can prevent eighty percent of chronic disease and improve longevity.

FOOD AND CHILDHOOD DEVELOPMENT

Our formative years are critical for growth and development and establishing essential physical and mental abilities. From birth, we start a relationship with food on a physical, mental, social, and emotional level. The substance, quantity, quality, timing, and nutrient components of every meal should be investigated to ensure children get the good stuff and in sufficient quantities.

We know the power of the social influence of food: it's how we celebrate, connect, support, and show love. This starts in childhood. Through being part of family meals, the social component of eating and our relationship with food expands.

Little people learn through exploration but also through imagination and mimicry. The child begins to mimic food and eating choices, patterns, and behaviours modelled by older siblings, parents, peers, and caregivers. The structure of family meals sets limits for little children as they learn to eat by themselves, but the entire experience can have lifelong impacts. Was food accessible? Was it enough? Or was it survival of the fittest, first come, first fed?

The accessibility of particular foods, modelling, media exposure, and feeding interactions shape a child's eating behaviour and food preferences far beyond the feeding chair.[45] For example, my own children cannot just eat anything and anywhere. They always have something to say about food served to them outside our home. They'll say something along the lines of, "It was too oily" or "It was too healthy," just because of how I have nurtured them foodwise from the day they were born. To that effect, they have since rejected school dinners and prefer a homemade, packed lunch.

Eating problems established in childhood can be temporary, such as an intolerance for a certain grain or fruit, but emotional and social development may be

---

[45] www.child-encyclopedia.com/child-nutrition/according-experts/feeding-behaviour-infants-and-young-children-and-its-impact-child

impacted during late childhood, adolescence, and adulthood. Research has found that obesity, cardiovascular disease, diabetes, and behavioural problems occur more frequently in children with a history of early childhood feeding problems.

Overeating. In countries like the US, the prevalence of overweight children and childhood obesity increased to 10.4% in two- to five-year-olds, 15.3% in six- to eleven-year-olds, and 15.5% in twelve- to nineteen-year-olds. These children are predisposed to conditions such as diabetes, hypertension, orthopaedic ailments, and sleep problems as well as poor self-esteem, dysfunctional body image, isolation, psychological maladjustment, depression, and eating disorders.

Stigmatization can start as early as pre-school as they are teased and rejected for being overweight and unable to join in games and sports. If parents don't handle it well, by severely restricting their diet, their children may develop eating disorders.

Poor appetite and failure to gain sufficient weight. Genetics, food, and activity levels affect how children gain weight. Toddlers would often rather play than eat, so it's important to seek guidance on age and environment-related milestones so that appropriate adjustments are made.

Feeding behaviour problems. There comes a point in our life when we don't want to be fed. Well, perhaps not until much later, when it becomes romantic for our partner to cook for and feed us. But as we leave infancy, we want to reach for our own plates and cutlery, and most often it ends up on the table, floor, or all over our clothing.

When parents don't have the patience to let children learn how to feed themselves, or if they punish them for not eating fast enough or refusing to eat what's on their plates, it creates long-term problems. Food phobias or a post-traumatic feeding disorder may result from a painful episode like choking or a difficult experience associated with a food-induced allergic reaction, such as near-coma from peanuts or a painful rash from seafood. If mealtimes were conflict scenes, we may also associate being fed with fear and discomfort.

Across human history, and particularly in underdeveloped and developing countries, undernutrition and food scarcity have been major threats to children's survival, and parental feeding practices have evolved in response to these threats. These feeding practices, which include behaviours such as providing large portions of palatable foods and encouraging children to eat, are still pervasive in most cultures, despite the fact that in many regions the balance has shifted from food scarcity to food excess, and over-consumption has become a new threat.[46]

In societies where physical constitution is often equated with status, a "bigger is better" mentality may also influence parental feeding practices regarding portion sizes and energy density of foods offered to eating behaviour and weight status.

Since children learn from others, they learn about food by observing the eating behaviours modelled by others. Similar to the research described around social media and sustenance in Chapter Two, studies reveal that children's intake of fruits, vegetables, and milk increased after observing adults consuming these foods. When children observed the eating behaviour of their peers, the effect was similar.

Positive social modelling is an indirect yet effective practice for promoting healthier diets in children, and parents can use this tactic to their advantage. There are many television programmes and online content promoting children eating good food. Children should be exposed to this more frequently. Franchises like McDonald's, KFC, Wimpy, and the drive-through "fries, shake, and a toy" menus creates a whole new set of problems for parents, but prevention *is* the plan.

------

[46] https://www.ncbi.nlm.nih.gov/pmc/articles/PMC2678872/

Childhood cognitive development involves the maturation of attention, memory, learning, and perception. During these years, optimal brain development has been shown to be associated with better academic ability. Cognitive development is vulnerable to dietary deficiencies.[47]

Child malnutrition could take the form of both under-nutrition and over-nutrition, both deficiency diseases caused by inadequate nutrition. Not having enough food (under-nutrition) results in children having less energy and lower interest for learning, which negatively impacts intellectual development and academic performance. It also impacts physical growth and maturation, so growth rate, body weight, and height could be inadequate.

While malnutrition is often associated with emaciated bodies, we now recognise that obesity is another form of malnutrition. While bodies may become bigger, the diet typically contains low-nutrient foods alongside high fat and high carbohydrate content. Paediatric obesity is on the rise, with its concomitant increased risk of developing heart-related diseases in adolescence and adulthood. The social and emotional impacts of obesity are far-reaching; their confidence

---

[47] www.ausmed.com/cpd/articles/nutrition-for-children.

and fitness during physical activities puts growth and development at a disadvantage.

TIPS AND GUIDELINES FOR CHILDHOOD DEVELOPMENT

With childhood nutrition, the dishing up is often an uphill battle, as children might prefer foods that look good but lack nutritional value. Vegetables often don't make it to their favourite list, unless you can skilfully mask or pulverise them into pizza toppings, soups, and pastas. Furthermore, you want to limit allergies and inflammation. Children need energy to deal with school, play, and social activities they may be involved in, and with longer school days and after-care as parents work longer hours, planning and preparation are key to success.

HEALTHY FOOD OPTIONS

The following are good choices for growing children:

* Lean protein from poultry, beans, seafood, nuts, and seeds are easy to prepare and pack.

* Fresh, canned, or frozen fruits and vegetables are also great daily additions. The good ones are without added fats or sugars, and wholegrain foods such as breads, cereals, and pastas high in fibre help them with digestion and provide slow-release energy sources.

* Healthy dairy products such as milk, cheese, and yoghurt.

Children's TV networks are flooded with adverts for colourful food associated with superheroes and superpowers, but you need to limit their intake of added and refined sugars, refined grains, sodium, trans fats, saturated fats, and foods low in nutrients. These foods keep them hungry through empty calories and are often addictive.

It's critical to get directions from your healthcare team, especially around timing for moving from liquids to solids, when babies can start having dairy products and so forth. For creating sustainable healthy eating habits, consider the following:

* Teach children the importance of good nutrition as early as possible. The more they understand nutrition, the more excited they will be about eating healthy.
* Model the right eating behaviours so it becomes "the way our family acts around good food."
* Product lines for children need particular attention as they are advertised as energy-boosting and health-giving options, but in reality hide hundreds of toxic ingredients behind the cute cartoon cutouts.

* Read those ingredient labels with a magnifying glass.

* Focus on the nutrient content, but also pay close attention to portion sizes.

* Half of their plate should be colourful fruits and vegetables. Fresh foods trump processed foods, so find interesting ways to make good meals more exciting without losing its nutritional value

* Offer water or unsweetened dairy products, avoiding sugary, sweetened drinks and milkshakes.

* Variety helps them consume a balance of nutrients without getting bored. Find a vegetable or fruit they like, and experiment with different ways to add it into their meals and snacks.

FOOD AND MENTAL WELLNESS

One may not immediately make the link between food and mood, but chemistry and energy are foregrounded through numerous studies. In fact, the medical field didn't do so, either, but today we have a branch of medicine called Nutritional Psychiatry, and this is a telling development.

This research has found, among other links, that a well-balanced diet improves clarity and alertness, focus, and attention span. Food can improve our mood, increase energy (or deplete it), and make us think more clearly (or conversely render our cognition cloudy). A poor diet has been shown to aggravate and even cause stress and depression.[48]

Highly addictive processed foods flooding our diets stimulate the dopamine brain centres associated with pleasure and reward, so when we're having a bad day, we're more likely to reach for something sugary, dense, and unhealthy. It doesn't last long, and soon enough, we've finished packets, pots, and bottles of feel-good without confronting our true feelings or having a head clear enough to devise a solution.

Sugar and processed foods lead to inflammation throughout our bodies and brains, potentially contributing to mood disorders, including anxiety and depression. When we're not at the top of our game we often eat too much or too little. We often don't feel like cooking a nutritious meal, and I know of those who would live on coffee, energy drinks, alcohol, or cigarettes when they're feel stressed or mourning.

Steamed vegetables, fruit skewers and herby salads are highly unlikely joy-restoration options when we feel overwhelmed, doubled over with menstrual pain, or finding Plan Next when the love of our life has walked out. However, when we establish healthy eating as part

---

[48] www.sutterhealth.org/health/nutrition/eating-well-for-mental-health.

of a holistic lifestyle of meaning and positive energy, we navigate the low points with more poise and balance. This way, a bad day or weekend doesn't become weeks, months, and years of self-destruction. With a strong constitution and self-care practices like exercise, meditation, prayer, worship, and supportive relationships, chances are the tough days won't bring us to our worst. It's about the little decisions that add up and help us build resilience.

FOOD AND MOOD

If your blood sugar drops you might feel tired, irritable and depressed. Eating regularly and choosing foods that release energy slowly will help to keep your sugar levels steady. Slow-release energy foods include: pasta, rice, oats, wholegrain bread and cereals, nuts, and seeds.

Research provides evidence of a strong connection between our gut and brain, organs that are physically linked via the vagus nerve for sending messages to each other. The gut is able to influence emotional behaviour in the brain, while the brain can also change bacteria in the gut, thereby producing an array of neurochemicals that the brain uses for the regulation of physiological and mental processes, including mood. It's believed 95% of the body's supply of serotonin, a mood stabilizer, is produced by gut bacteria. Stress is thought to suppress beneficial gut bacteria.[49]

Serotonin helps regulate sleep and appetite, mediate moods, and inhibit pain. What's more, the function of these neurons—and the production of neurotransmitters like serotonin—is highly influenced by the billions of "good" bacteria making up the intestinal microbiome. These bacteria protect the lining of the intestines, providing a strong barrier against toxins and "bad" bacteria; they restrict inflammation, improve nutrient absorption, and activate neural pathways between gut and brain.[50]

Some guidelines to sustain energy:

- ➢ Start the day with a good breakfast.
- ➢ Eating smaller portions throughout the day keeps insulin levels balanced.
- ➢ Avoid the foods that spike and drop sugar levels, like alcohol, processed food, and refined sugars.
- ➢ Get enough fluid; the brain needs water for concentration.

---

[49] www.sutterhealth.org/health/nutrition/eating-well-for-mental-health.

[50] www.health.harvard.edu/blog/nutritional-psychiatry-your-brain-on-food-201511168626.

➢ Maintain some structure and control by creating a healthy shopping list you can stick to, and don't shop when you're hungry.

➢ Pump up the protein: it contains the chemicals that regulate our thoughts and feelings, as well as keeping us fuller for longer

➢ Maintain gut health: this further supports emotional balance through fiber, fluids, fruits, vegetables wholegrains, beans, pulses, live yoghurt and other probiotics, and adequate exercise. It takes time to find the right combinations to stabilize the gut, but remain patient. It may also require forms of relaxation to enhance it.

➢ Beware the brew: caffeine is a stimulant, which means a quick burst of energy that can be followed by feeling anxious and depressed, disrupt sleep, or even produce withdrawal symptoms, if you stop suddenly. The decaffeinated variants of tea, coffee, or soda are preferable. You might feel noticeably better quite quickly, if you drink less caffeine or avoid it altogether.

➢ Know the fats: Our brain needs fatty acids (such as omega-3 and omega-6) to keep it working optimally. Instead of avoiding all fats, choose to eat the right ones easily found in oily fish, poultry, nuts, olive and sunflower oils, sunflower or pumpkin seeds, avocados, milk, yoghurt, unprocessed cheese, and eggs.

➢ Your health practitioner will guide you on diet, especially when you're on medications like lithium and anti-anxiety medications, because these come with serious contraindications even for food and other medicines.

➢ Make meal times a special time to relax and focus on the nutrition you have that is rebuilding you. It's helpful to pay attention to how consuming certain foods makes you feel, in the moment, but also afterwards.

➢ If you find you overeat when stressed, it may be helpful to stop what you're doing when the urge to eat arises and write down your feelings. By doing this, you may discover what's really bothering you. If you undereat, it may help to schedule five or six smaller meals instead of three large ones.

➢ If you find it hard to control your eating habits, whether you're eating too much or too little, your health may be in jeopardy. If this is the case, you should seek professional counselling. Asking for help is never a sign of weakness or failure, especially in situations too difficult to handle alone.

I learned that whenever I start a detox or begin eating clean for at least ten days, I feel renewed, and this lasts as long as I keep my diet free of refined sugars, processed food and drinks, and white flour treats. As soon as I reintroduce these foods back into my diet, my eyes feel scratchy, I often have sinus-type headaches, and in no time, I feel sluggish and uncomfortable. And inexplicably moody. Maintenance is key; don't undo the gains you make through healthy, nourishing food and all the positive behaviours that go with it.

WEIGHT LOSS AND FOOD

This section contains no miracle weight-loss formulae, simply because none exist. Considering the obesity pandemic on the planet, it's safe to say none of the scientific endeavours in the world's best laboratories of our time have produced a magic pill or elixir without side-effects. Without a holistic health perspective, sustainable weight loss isn't possible anyway. Instead, the focus is on self-care and a look at the great, nutritious options available in Africa.

There's simply too much misinformation about health and lifestyle. There's no one-size-fits-all formula. Skinny has been equated with healthy. Some people look fit, but thanks to genetics, they're ingesting inordinate amount of unhealthy food and snacks and may be sleep deprived or constantly stressed. They, too, may not realise how much trouble they're in, because being whole means exactly that: getting all our life dimensions into alignment.

When you're exercising to get away from home and a bad relationship, it isn't ideal. If you're forcing yourself to eat lettuce due to pathological fear of being overweight, there's something heavy in there. All the cruciferous vegetables cannot save us from unresolved crises and trauma. Health and happiness go together, and quick fixes tend to lead us to focus on one area at the expense of the others. We need to feed mind, body, and soul; this means immersing ourselves in the things that set our soul on fire: causes, relationships, hobbies, spiritual connections, and lifelong learning.

Finding the things to put on our plates may be relatively easier, but we also need to think about why, when, how often, and with whom we eat. We need to figure out what our excess weight or baggage is and dump it. Not all calories are created equal; each can have vastly different effects on your hunger, hormones, and how much get metabolised at a time.

Weight loss in Africa is more difficult because of the carbohydrate-rich nature of African foods, but the continent is filled with many diverse, healthy options. It simply takes a little effort and maybe even a little trial and error to find the right weight loss foods.[51] These are some of the most popular and very versatile weight-loss options:

African star apple (Udara): rich in fibre, vitamin C, and antioxidants; single servings contain about 67 calories, are very filling, and serve as a great snack, especially during pregnancy.

Papaya: incredibly nutrient-dense; one cup of cubed papaya contains 60 calories with 3g of fibre. Papaya extract could reduce total cholesterol and LDL cholesterol.

Baobab fruit: fresh or powdered baobab fruit offers vitamin C, minerals, and antioxidants; it has been shown to reduce hunger pangs.

Avocado: contains healthy fats, water, potassium, and fibre. They are high in monounsaturated oleic acid, the same fat found in olive oil. Studies show its fat content increases carotenoid antioxidant absorption from vegetables 2.6-15-fold.

Tomato: packed with key vitamins, minerals, and antioxidants; low in calories.

Unripe plantain: green unripe plantain is high in resistant starch and less sweet than bananas. One study

---

[51] www.healthfulwonders.com/weight-loss-foods-in-africa/.

linked it to reduced abdominal fat and improved insulin sensitivity; also, feeling fuller for longer advantage. Versatile and prepared in different ways in Africa, including frying, boiling, or roasting.

Oats: full of fibre and protein.

Wild African rice (Ofada rice): incredibly nutritious, it is full of fibre and resistant starch, which enhances satiety and prevents overeating. To be eaten in moderation.

Pigeon peas: a highly nutritious weight-loss legume rich in healthy carbohydrates, protein, fat, and fibre. One cup offers about 203 calories. It's good in stews and salads.

Cowpeas (Black-eyed peas): incredibly nutrient-dense, they're great added to rice, salads, or porridge.

Bambara groundnuts (Okpa): high in fibre, protein, and carbohydrates. They're typically made into dumplings in African cuisine or roasted as snacks.

Whole Eggs: nutrient-dense foods in a low-calorie package, they increase feelings of satiety for long periods.

Coconut oil and olive oil: rich in healthy fats and known to burn belly fat. One study in forty women showed that supplementation with coconut oil helped the women lose abdominal fat.[52]

Potatoes: loaded with potassium, and contains most necessary nutrients and dietary fiber. However, always remember to eat them in moderation, as they are high in carbohydrates.

Taro (cocoyam): this root vegetable is rich in resistant starch and makes amazing additions to stews, tasty snacks, and healthy thickening agents for soups.

Roselle (Hibiscus tea): Hibiscus tea is rich in antioxidants and enzymes that help in weight loss. One twelve-week study showed that hibiscus extract reduced body weight, body fat, body mass index, and hip-to-waist ratio in thirty-six overweight individuals.

Green Tea: Green tea is a zero-calorie beverage rich in caffeine and antioxidants called catechins. In a study, green tea extract was believed to facilitate rapid weight loss and burn belly fat in individuals who drank green tea and exercised for twenty-five minutes.

Black Coffee: Black coffee is a zero-calorie beverage. It is rich in caffeine that helps boost your metabolism and makes you lose weight quickly.

---

[52] Carney, Jake. "Rethink: Why Coconut Oil Kills Belly Fat." www.stanfordchiropractic.com/blogs/rethink/why-coconut-oil-kills-belly-fat.html.

Pure Cocoa Drink (not the sweetened ones that make hot chocolate): This is a wonderful fat-blaster, rich in fibre, flavonoids, and vitamins.

VITALITY TIPS

> ➢ *Daily choices add up to longevity; we can avoid lifestyle diseases.*
>
> ➢ *The food and eating behaviours established in childhood stay with us throughout our lives (for better or worse).*
>
> ➢ *Development doesn't necessarily mean progress for our species; we need to interact with our natural and spiritual surroundings with consciousness and wisdom.*
>
> ➢ *Many of the Western diets are making their way through socio-economics, but we have so many great and healthy options on the African continent.*

CHAPTER FIVE

FOOD AND SOCIETY

Socio-Cultural Impact of Cooking and Eating

Modern society faces some challenges around food, among them the fact that we seldom reflect on its origins. Our fast-paced world, full of takeout and mindless eating while focusing more on devices, means we're not registering the food and not truly connecting to our source, our nourishment, and one another. Fortunately, there is increasingly more attention being paid to regaining the value of healthy eating and connecting. Small changes can bring about remarkable health benefits.

WORK AND FOOD

We are constantly rushing and have a malnourishing mania around multitasking. Commonplace are working meetings, working lunches, signing proposals, and deals over dinner. We're trying to save time, but at what cost?

Enjoyable, soulful practices are often placed on the back burner, so we often miss out on the taste, texture, aromas, and flavours of our food. We may be fuelled up, but it isn't the most fulfilling experience.

FOOD, CULTURE, AND IDENTITY

Food represents a mechanism for forming ethnic, cultural, and social identity. It's often the quickest way to make contact with and even navigate different cultures, given that eating the food of others seems easier than learning their language. Globalization means that cuisines are making their way across the world at a tremendous pace, which provides us the opportunity for bonding and sharing experiences.

Food and how it is shared have special significance for individuals, groups, and broader society. Food includes a symbolic and social meaning that reaches beyond its nutritional value and the physical need to refuel. What and how to eat are regarded as selections of products and conventions with a unique meaning and identity.

The table where meals are shared, for example, defines roles and relationships. In the past, this may relate to gender-role differences in some societies (with one seated and the other on their feet, serving) or the monarch who eats alone or the sequence in which food is served. Similarly, sharing food, or who gets which piece or portion as opposed to another, is not casual; rather, it is the translation of relationships of power and prestige within a family or group.

The quality and quantity of food is an expression of culture, culinary tradition, and social status. How and how much someone eats derive from and reveal the social standing of that individual, e.g., eating with cutlery that used in a particular sequence means something to some, while in other cultures everyone eats by hand. There was a time when meat was more expensive than fruit, vegetables, or grains, and the more meat you had in a meal, the richer you were. Or it could be about the quality or grade of the meat. In modern times, grains traditionally are associated with peasantry and rustic living; these days, though, millet, rye, and barley are making a prominent and not inexpensive comeback.

In some traditions, the giving and slaughtering of livestock were key to binding families, as part of debt settlement or as dowry gifts. Of course, there are millions the world over who don't eat meat at all, guided by strict spiritual or religious prescripts. As with most things, though, these methods and mindsets evolve over time.

Another key consideration is the link between eating habits and environmental sustainability. Agricultural activity is responsible for producing more than a third of the total global annual greenhouse-gas emissions. Pesticides and fertilizer overuse have resulted in large-scale land degradation. Rearing of livestock can cause even more problems. Massive rates of urbanization across the world have further impacted sustainability, and changes in human diet have had huge health and social impacts. Increased knowledge about lifestyle diseases and nutrition as medicine will potentially prevent further incidents.

The other big socio-cultural impact is through advertising, smart branding, and selective disclosure. With more advocacy and greater legal implications, food manufacturers now experience some pressure to improve their processes and publicly declare their ingredients and sources. With food activists, scientific research, and climate change pressure, there will probably be competition to offer more healthy foods and brands that value variety and emphasize eating as an experience.

With a society doing everything in public and wanting feedback on it, social media has become a menu, a creativity hub, and a rolling photo album smartly logging memories and digital footprints, so it's no surprise that our meals and eating habits, preferences, and locations have made it to cyberspace. Meals are suddenly trending, and diet success stories are as commonplace as exotic vacations. This practice will continue to influence our relationship with food, as a species.

Breaking Bread: Food as Family and Communion

Many forever relationships start with food. Or, more specifically, with an invitation to eat or drink together. Going out for a drink, coffee or a meal has even come to signify mutual attraction and interest and may involve a fair amount of preparation and anticipation to make a good first impression.

In time, we come to celebrate milestones with meals. Making favourite meals for end of term or birthdays, for graduations or promotions. If there are spiritual or religious celebrations, these often involve food, too, like Christmas, Eid, or Thanksgiving. Loved ones get together after the rituals around a table or fireplace; the smells, flavours, speeches, prayers, incantations, and laughter are what we remember, even as, hours later, our stomachs may remind us about a much-needed top-up or refill.

Some of my favourite memories are of spending time with my children. And, through grace, we add to these daily. They have been through so much in their young lives, and I'm often overwhelmed by their resilience, as they've grown into awesome, kind, respectful, able young people who are passionately pursuing their dreams. Meal times are especially important to us:

preparing for it, having fun with new recipes, and getting the table ready. And after all that, sharing a prayer and just *being,* safe and together.

I'm sure the impact of COVID has changed the way we see life and death, and perhaps more so the brevity and uncertainty of our human lifetime. Sharing a meal strengthens the bonds that unite us as family, friends, and community. It's one of our simplest structures of belonging. It is one of the reasons the separation and isolation demanded throughout the lockdowns were particularly hard for many. It has prevented us from gathering and dining with those we care about, alongside the real fear of never seeing them again.

In other homes, those who prioritised meal times together were faced with disruption as partners and children were stuck in various locations and locked down until further notice. During extreme lockdowns, weddings, anniversaries, and birthday parties were celebrated virtually, with each participant sharing in the festivities with their plate and glass of something. It felt lonely and a desperate stab at being festive, but it was our attempt to still be together while being apart. Certainly, an interesting time in history.

The elderly and destitute were isolated, some with meagre supplies, and many battled as food couldn't reach them. Jobs and incomes were swiftly lost. In some homes, meals were a time of blessing; in other homes, a battlefield.

We cannot take anything for granted, and so a meal shared can become a time of decompression, just sharing the day's highs and lows, or a chance for savouring the flavours that bring up pleasant memories and dreams of places we want to visit. It is the time of appreciation for a labour of love and, sometimes, of creativity as something on the plate inspires us to a next best recipe or idea.

We are what we eat physically and emotionally through the chemicals and compounds, but eating together also adds a social dimension, bringing a sense of belonging and highlighting a shared space.

COOKING: GENETIC SIGNIFICANCE FOR OUR SPECIES

We may take cooking for granted nowadays, as we easily heat a meal or utilise a myriad of cooking utensils, but the prehistoric humans didn't start their relationship with food in the form we enjoy it now. And cooking fundamentally changed homo sapiens as a species.

Up to the point when fire was discovered, humans interacted with nature simply in an "eat or be eaten" capacity. From this evolved at least five reasons to cook food:

1) To improve the taste
2) To render it safer for consumption
3) To improve digestibility
4) To enhance its appearance (we eat with all our senses), and
5) To alter its texture[53]

Interestingly, in ancient Greece, the words "cook," "butcher," and "priest" were the same: *mageiros,* which shares its etymological root with the word "magic." Cooking is more than simply roasting or boiling something to eat. Over the centuries, cooking evolved into an art (I was seriously enthralled by my culinary course) and sometimes even into a religious practice or primary outreach endeavour such as soup kitchens.

French anthropologist Claude Lévi-Strauss suggested cooking food using fire was "the invention that made human beings human." Before utilizing the practice of cooking, food (particularly meat) was eaten raw, spoiled, or even rotten. The application of fire brought about a decisive change. Cooking symbolically marked a transition from nature to culture and thence to society, given that while *raw* is natural in origin, *cooked* food is both cultural and social.

-----

[53] https://melanniesvobodasnd.org/the-spirituality-of-cooking/

Cooking as an Expression of Love and Affection

I grew up subscribing to the adage that the kitchen was the heart of the home. It was the place we congregated for meals, and I know, for some of my friends who came from huge families, their cultural impacts affected where and how they ate, along with particular gender roles (e.g., fathers ate with boys, and girls with their mothers in a separate section of the kitchen).

But everyone passed through the kitchen at least once a day. If it had a coal stove or fireplace, it was the heater, the pantry, the snack box, the library, and the study. Cooking and baking provide great bonding experiences, with the added bonus of something scrumptious at the end. Some friends and family see the kitchen as the real congregating space, where good and bad news is mediated through bottomless cups of tea. It can get messy, and it can get cleaned up with minimum fuss.

These days, the little ones end up doing their homework at the kitchen table or counter, and it's not unlikely to find the family's notice board plastered across the fridge. While some rooms may be off-limits to others, the kitchen is the source of cross-paths and daily meeting. It's Home Central for sure, and it can be the place where the hustle and bustle is abandoned to turn attention to what it's meant to be: a hub of great food and good conversation. And, in those moments of inspiration, a culinary laboratory where you take your knowledge of nutrition and rustle up health-giving meals and drinks.

I have also found that food serves as expression and engagement. When I first attended our church, being unknown, I discovered how baking a cake got me noticed. It certainly wasn't my intention, but in time, I was known as the Cake Lady. Something so simple created a case for connection, and we never looked back.

Furthermore, cooking demonstrates nurturing. Through our food evolution, so many new roles and industries came about, even in the field of holistic and mental health. "Giving to others fills us in so many ways," suggests Michal AviShai, a culinary arts therapist (Doesn't that sound like an interesting profession?) "And even more so when it's cooking, because feeding fulfils a survival need, so our feeling of fulfilment comes not only from the good of the act of giving, but also the fact that we have 'helped' in some very primal way. We have given fuel."[54]

Such acts potentially improve a sense of trust, meaning, purpose, belonging, and social intimacy—all

---

[54] Thompson, Julie R. "The Very Real Psychological Benefits of Cooking for Other People." *Huffington Post.* 17 Oct 2017.

of which have been linked to increased happiness, lowered depression, and greater positive overall wellbeing. Cooking for others also helps bond us to our loved ones and fellow humans. Michael Pollan wrote, "Cooking gave us the meal and the meal gave us civilization." And feeling connected to others can have great effects, like living a longer life and increased happiness.

When we cook for someone, it creates a bond, sustains the relationship, and on the most basic level, enhances their health and survival. This causes us to flourish as social beings designed to serve. Just like with food and water, for us, cooking builds and affirms primary social connections whilst meeting our most basic needs. Cooking, essentially and quite easily, deepens these connections.

If I haven't said it enough, cooking is a form of self-care, and I cannot stress this enough, because you regain control of what goes into your system. Preparing your food is a commitment to feeding your body, but it is also an investment in you, in a busy world. It may be delicious and nutritious, but it also simply says, "I Matter." And if you're good or getting good in the kitchen, it also does wonders for your confidence. Being able to create a feast with leftovers or creating bounty off seemingly empty shelves takes some ingenuity.

Cooking also makes or brings up memories, which isn't really something you think about when you're out shopping or your stomach is grumbling. But the sights, sounds, and textures of preparing or enjoying a good meal can connect you to special moments and people, even those no longer with you. An aroma can conjure up a scene completely buried in your subconscious, and out of nowhere, a childhood friend or grandparent feels really close. Or you recall a time when you promised you'd have a better life than when you were struggling, and here you stand at the sink or stove, hearing the children get ready for the meal, and your dreams have come true. All from the aromas of an herb or spice or the gurgling of a hearty stew. That is magical and, in some ways, therapeutic. All the more reason to cook and eat mindfully.

COOKING AND EATING FOR SPIRITUALITY: WHAT THE BIBLE SAYS ABOUT FOOD

Since earliest times, food has been an integral part of spiritual life. In ancestral traditions, food was connected with sacred ceremonial processes such as song, storytelling, and drumming.[55] Through the ages, cooking was regarded as a shared activity that united families

---

[55] www.naturalhealthmag.com.au/content/discover-relationship-between-spirituality-and-nutrition.

and communities, as they prepared and shared their meals together.

While a bit of that may have changed as we move to cramped urban living or live in secluded complexes and estates, we can still purposely cultivate a connection between our cooking spaces and reclaim the joyous celebration of food and life.

"Our modern lifestyles have separated us from the most basic involvement in our day-to-day needs, and part of coming back to ourselves, nature, and spirituality is through nourishing ourselves, and this happens in the kitchen," says Bahareh Hosseini, educator with Wise Earth Ayurveda and a Chinese medicine practitioner. "According to ancient Vedic tradition, the kitchen is the most sacred space in the house, because that's where health, longevity, and nourishment are restored to the family, and through cooking practices we're able to get back in touch with those elements," says Hosseini. "It's also a very divine feminine aspect of spirituality to be in the kitchen and involved in cooking."[56]

There are several Biblical scriptures referencing the connection between food and spirituality that deeply resonate with me.

---

[56] claritywellness.co

Genesis 1:29: "And God said, behold, I have given you every plant-yielding seed that is on the face of all the earth, and every tree with seed in its fruit. you shall have them for food."

Genesis 9:3: "Every moving thing that lives shall be food for you. And as I gave you the green plants, I give you everything."

John 6:35: "Jesus said to them, 'I am the bread of life; whoever comes to me shall not hunger, and whoever believes in me shall never thirst.'"

1 Timothy 4:4-5:"For everything created by God is good, and nothing is to be rejected if it is received with thanksgiving, for it is made holy by the word of God and prayer."

1 Corinthians 10:31: "So whether you eat or drink or whatever you do, do all for the glory of God."

Ecclesiastes 9:7: "Go eat your bread with joy, and drink your wine with a merry heart, for God has already approved what you do."

In these Scriptures, it is clear that, through cooking and eating, we make a spiritual connection with our higher power or the Source, if you would like to call Him that. I call Him God, and whenever I grow, harvest, prepare, or sit down to eat food, I am overwhelmed with humility and gratitude.

Human beings have to eat and drink to survive. When we give thanks for each meal, it means we are connecting with our God at least once a day through prayer and thanksgiving. This is critical for balance and a meaningful-centred life.

Slowing down, not taking things for granted, preparing an extra plate just in case someone pops in, sending the children out with a food parcel to someone destitute, or packing an extra sandwich for someone at work or school are all ways of becoming more conscious of ourselves, our surroundings, and reaching out to those around us. Many are crying out for their next morsel. In this age of technology and innovation, many are still malnourished and dying of starvation.

I cannot think of the link between food and spirituality without thinking of mindfulness. "Bread for the World" by Bernadette Farrell is a hymn that reminds me of the fundamental Christian tenet, "loving God above all and our neighbour as we do ourselves."

We have physical and spiritual hunger that needs satisfying on a daily basis. As the lyrics go, those of us blessed to receive have a responsibility to give to others, whether it's a piece of bread or forgiveness or a kind word. That's how we become conscious of being part of something greater and realise that it is a privilege to be able to give to others.

Cooking from scratch can be just as sacred a ritual as any. When you cook food in your home, your personal energy is infused into it, and you control that energy and can then infuse intentions into the food, as well. But because your personal energy goes into it, your emotional state is important, as it will be reflected in the meal.[57] Making a shopping list and taking a bus, cab, or a drive to get the ingredients, having enough money to pay for it, and getting safely back to the cutting board are all magical acts. On the surface, it may look like a chore, but if mindfully executed, it changes the game completely.

Perhaps you like cooking to some good music, or perhaps you feel more connected to the process and silence is the best accompaniment to your slicing, shredding, or rinsing. Going into the garden or vegetable patch may be one of the most spiritual cooking acts yet. You become part of the ecosystem in an intentional way, reaping what you've sown and lovingly tended for weeks and months, and now the next step is creating something needful to be enjoyed by others.

In *Heaven All Around Us: God in Everyday Life,* Simon Carey Holt describes the powerful religious experience of leafing through his mother's cookbook. He writes,

---

[57] www.goodwitchkitchen.net/eating-as-a-spiritual-practice/.

"When I hold my mother's recipes, I understand better who I am, where I am from, and, in part, who I aspire to be. ... This tattered old book is a testament to her priestly service ... She served me and fed me.... In eating her food, I was nourished, enfolded, forgiven, enriched."[58]

The Zen priest Edward Epse Brown wrote a book entitled *No Recipe: Cooking as a Spiritual Practice,* wherein he outlines the profound connection between cooking and spiritual life. He writes, "Making your love manifest, transforming your spirit, good heart, and able hands into food, is a great undertaking—one that will nourish you in the doing, in the offering, and in the eating." Throughout my research, I discovered that the spiritual state we are in while preparing food translates to those who partake of it. Even a rushed evening meal after a busy day and rough traffic can be infused with care and focus.

We were taught to pray for our food in the home or kindergarten even as toddlers. And it sounded funny or cute as we recited or sang, focusing more on the tune than the intention. This visual stays with me, and with the insights of adulthood, I can focus my attention on the words and the range of my prayer. We can be thankful that, despite all the human horrors and natural

---

[58] https://melanniesvobodasnd.org/the-spirituality-of-cooking/

disasters, forces have come together: sun, rain, soil, fire, irrigation, human and mechanical labour, distribution, and generations of recipes and ideas with our ability to create something. That is a miracle in itself. Hence, we bless the hands that prepare the food, not just the last lap from fire to plate, but each one along the way.

SOME TIPS FOR ENHANCING A SPIRITUAL CONNECTION WITH FOOD

* ❖ Using your knowledge of various nutrients, **choose foods with a specific purpose** in mind, e.g., anti-ageing, detox, or inflammation-busting.

* ❖ **Make it a mood.** As you cook and eat, picture the end game. Avoid the temptation to read emails or scroll through social media; instead, bring attention back to the cutting, stirring, and measuring or the wonderful wafts from your culinary creation.

* ❖ **Acknowledge your nutritional sources.** Preparation is a good moment to think about where the food actually came from: where it was cultivated or harvested. There may be something significant about the recipe—a family secret or a fun creation that happened over a memorable childhood holiday. Perhaps it makes you feel proud or homesick. Perhaps the cutting board was a gift. It's a good time to practise gratitude.

❖ **Share a meal.** Sharing a meal with those you love is an enchanted experience all on its own, and it doesn't have to be an elaborate ceremony to be magical. Adding a few candles or making some effort with a tablecloth is enough to communicate that the meal and company matter. Perhaps some weekdays are special meal days, e.g., the usual with pudding or champagne or a special brand of coffee. Or no washing of dishes, children treat parents, or vice versa. It doesn't have to be elaborate or expensive to be special.

VITALITY TIPS

➤ *Find simple ways to slow down and take stock while cooking or eating.*

➤ *Consider whether cooking is a chore, a necessary nuisance, or does it bring excitement to create new ways to bring more of you to the table.*

➤ *Reflect on childhood memories that cooking or dining bring up for you.*

➤ *Consider how catering to large groups of people, e.g., a family gathering or celebration, makes you feel.*

CHAPTER SIX

FOOD AND STRESS: A RECIPE FOR DISASTER

Human beings can experience positive stress, called *eustress*, and negative stress, the one we experience most often, called *distress*.

We need stress to stay alive. We need triggers so that we can take action. The alarm clock means something; the prospect of failing an exam propelling us to prepare and study means something. This gives us energy and can be most rewarding. Distress, on the other hand, is characterised by the feeling of being overwhelmed or unable to cope with mental, physical, or emotional pressure.

DEFINING STRESS

Stress is inevitable but manageable, and this is where self-care and diet come into play. It also strengthens stress-tolerance and resilience and prevents episodes of complete overwhelm.

Many different situations or life events can cause stress. It is often triggered when we experience something new, unexpected, or threatening to our sense of self, or when we feel we have little control over a situation.[59]

Stress affects our eating habits and even our food preferences. Numerous studies have shown that physical or emotional distress increases the intake of foods high in fat, sugar, or both, through high cortisol levels in combination with high insulin levels. Other research suggests that ghrelin, a "hunger hormone," may play a role.[60] Once ingested, fat- and sugar-filled foods seem to have a feedback effect that dampens stress-related responses and emotions. These "comfort" foods seem to counteract stress in the short-term and may contribute to people's stress-induced cravings for those foods.

To add insult to injury, overeating isn't the only stress-related behavior that can add pounds. Stressed

---

[59] www.mentalhealth.org.uk/a-to-z/s/stress.

[60] www.health.harvard.edu/staying-healthy/why-stress-causes-people-to-overeat#:~:text=In%20the%20short%20term%2C%20stress,temporarily%20puts%20eating%20on%20hold.

people also lose sleep, exercise less, and drink more alcohol, all of which can contribute to excess weight.

Harvard researchers have reported that work stress and other challenges correlate with weight gain, especially in those who were overweight to begin with. One theory is that overweight people have elevated insulin levels, and stress-related weight gain is more likely to occur in the presence of high insulin. How much cortisol people produce in response to stress may also factor into the stress–weight gain equation.

BITING OFF MORE THAN YOU CAN CHEW: VICIOUS CYCLES AND COPING

Stress can lead to unhealthy habits that negatively affect our health. For example, many people cope with stress by eating too much or by smoking, gambling, drinking, or engaging in other high-risk behaviours. These habits damage the body and create bigger problems in the long term, such as stealing to maintain a gambling habit or developing an eating disorder to deal with childhood trauma, abuse, or a distorted self-perception.

TASTE YOUR TRIGGERS: ENHANCING AWARENESS OF PHYSICAL SYMPTOMS

A huge part of stress management is self-awareness: knowing what, where, when, and who stresses you beyond your threshold. You can't fight an enemy if you can't accurately identify them. In physical terms, that means treating a symptom and not the root cause.

For example, a nosy, critical mother-in-law may trigger feelings of worthlessness or failure, so her visits may propel you to bad food or alcohol, which helps in the short term but doesn't address the real issue: what about her words or behaviour aggravate unresolved wounds? Worse still, alcohol and stress-eating quickly engage vicious cycles of negative emotions and self-destructive or dysfunctional behaviour.

We can be stressed by our interpretation (90%) of anything: it could be a job, constant fear of living in a crime-infested area, uncertainty about finances, children's safety or peer groups, a partner's dodgy behaviour, the inability to be assertive, or a midlife crisis. The goal is to anticipate stress and have healthy coping strategies and supports in place, before it brings our face to the pavement. If we land on our feet, it's easier to get back up.

STRESS, DIS-EASE, AND MEDICATION

When we experience stress, our bodies produce stress hormones that trigger a fight-or-flight response and activate our immune system. This design feature helps us respond quickly to dangerous situations. The problem is, over time, these hormones are as deadly as they can be helpful.

We need adrenaline and cortisol for short bursts, to scale walls, climb trees, win athletic feats, and get away from predators. But when they course through our systems for long periods, it becomes maladaptive, hence causing our cells to be damaged, organs to change shape, our mental health to be compromised over time, and it can kill us.

In essence we need to learn to manage the *On* and *Off* switches to our stress triggers, which we do through awareness, mindfulness, and loads of practice. Some people are better at managing stress than others, and genetics, personality, life histories, and general life perspective are all differentiating factors.

Psychological signs include difficulty concentrating, excessive worrying, anxiety, and memory problems

Emotional signs like anger, irritation, fluctuating moods, and unwarranted frustration

Physical signs include high blood pressure, weight loss or gain, frequent colds or recurring infections, and changes in menstrual cycles and sexual issues.

Behavioral signs are evidenced through poor self-care, abandoning things that bring fulfilment, or resorting to substances and distractions to cope.

Stress damages the body in a number of ways and, together with other diseases, brings us closer and faster to the grave.

Stress can have a short-term or long-term impact. It leads to a variety of symptoms, but chronic stress can take a serious toll on the body over time and have long-lasting health effects, including diabetes, heart disease, thyroid and sexual dysfunction, obesity, dental disease and ulcers. Physical symptoms to be aware of include inexplicable headaches, nausea, indigestion, digestive problems such as constipation, bloating, or diarrhoea, shallow breathing or hyperventilating, sweating, heart palpitations, and unrelated aches and pains.

Sleep deprivation is a common chronic stressor that potentially increases risk for obesity and metabolic diseases, including abdominal obesity, insulin resistance, hypertension, atherosclerosis; it predisposes sufferers to cardiovascular disease and type II diabetes.

In the short term, stress can shut down appetite. The nervous system sends messages to the adrenal glands and stops the kidneys from pumping out the hormone epinephrine/adrenaline. Epinephrine helps trigger the fight-or-flight response, making us so amped up, we don't feel like eating.

When stress persists, it's the opposite: the adrenal glands release cortisol, which increases appetite.

Basically, once the stress event is over, cortisol levels should fall, but if the stress response doesn't go away, non-stop eating or cravings for unhealthy foods persist.

TREATMENTS FOR STRESS

Typical treatments include psychotherapy, medication (anti-depressants, sleep aids, antacids, etc.), and complementary or alternative medicines, such as acupuncture, aromatherapy, massage, yoga, and forms of meditation. Understanding nutrients and food chemistry allows us to embrace more natural and sustainable solutions for stress-related conditions. It is said that life is 10% what happens to us and 90% how we respond, thus control and choices for a well-balanced life of learning and meaningfulness rest within our sphere, regardless of what is happening out there.

Life happens, and sometimes that ten percent is a rollercoaster of a rough ride, and believe me I've been through some spiritual fine-tuning (I even wrote a book about it). But there are mind-body-spirit practices that create more of a sense of coping and wellbeing, and there are some that plummet us into spirals of dysfunction.

If your goal is to lower stress, it is important to not skip meals, as they help balance blood sugar levels. Being in a chronic state of low blood sugar is stressful on your body and potentially increases cortisol, so maintaining a balanced blood sugar is critical.

HOLISTIC COOKING AND EATING

Chronic stress is often accompanied by anxiety, depression, anger, apathy, and alienation. Given the rewarding properties of food, it is suggested that hyperpalatable foods may serve as "comfort food" that acts as a form of self-medication to dispel unwanted distress. Individuals in negative affective states have been shown to favor the consumption of hedonically rewarding foods high in sugar and/or fat, whereas intake during happy states favor less palatable dried fruits.[61] Research studies have also shown that people with high cortisol reactivity needed to snack more in response to daily stressors.

When stress affects our appetite and waistline, we want to avoid a spiral by trading the short-term relief for a lifestyle overhaul. Sometimes, we need to help ourselves by completing getting rid of foods that trigger overeating or negative brain function, such as bad fat, sugary foods. The comfort foods have been notorious for being more hit-and-run than we need.

If you're trying to lower your stress levels, there are some garden variety staples: self-care, sleep

---

[61] www.ncbi.nlm.nih.gov/pmc/articles/PMC4214609/.

management, and exercise. And, of course, there are, according to dietitian Courtney Barth, certain foods that can help reduce your levels of cortisol, the primary hormone responsible for stress.[62]

Cortisol is responsible for regulating sleep cycles, reducing inflammation, increasing blood sugar, and managing how our body metabolises and uses carbohydrates, fats, and proteins, and controls blood pressure. It is commonly called the stress hormone because it is released by the adrenal gland when we are in a stressful situation or experiencing physical stress like inflammation.

In the long term, too much cortisol actually creates stress in your body, increasing inflammation and blood pressure—basically doing the opposite of the positive effects it brings in the short-term. Thus, managing stress is the number-one treatment for reducing cortisol levels. Focusing on cortisol-reducing foods is key.

The major focus to lower cortisol is to eat an anti-inflammatory diet. Simply dish up the whole foods and dump the processed options.

Chickpeas are packed with stress-fighting vitamins and minerals, including magnesium, potassium, B

---

[62] https://health.clevelandclinic.org/eat-these-foods-to-reduce-stress-and-anxiety/

vitamins, zinc, selenium, manganese, and copper. These delicious legumes are also rich in L-tryptophan, which your body needs to produce mood-regulating neurotransmitters. Diets rich in plant proteins like chickpeas may help boost brain health and improve mental performance.

Sunflower seeds are a rich source of vitamin E. This fat-soluble vitamin acts as a powerful antioxidant and is essential for mental health. Even in small amounts, it offers altered mood and depression remedies. It contains other stress-reducing nutrients, including magnesium, manganese, selenium, zinc, B vitamins, and copper.

Cruciferous vegetables like broccoli are some of the most concentrated food sources of some nutrients, including magnesium, vitamin C, and folate, that have been proven to combat depressive symptoms. Broccoli is also rich in sulforaphane, a sulphur compound that has neuroprotective properties and may offer calming and antidepressant effects.

Garlic is high in sulphur compounds that help increase levels of glutathione. This antioxidant is part of your body's first line of defense against stress and could potentially reduce symptoms of anxiety and depression.

Parsley is a nutritious herb rich in antioxidants. It is particularly rich in carotenoids, flavonoids, and volatile oils, all of which have powerful antioxidant properties.

Eggs are often referred to as nature's multivitamin because of their impressive nutrient profile. Whole eggs are packed with vitamins, minerals, amino acids, and antioxidants needed for a healthy stress response. They are rich in choline, which plays a significant role in brain health and may guard against stress.

Organ meats, including the heart, liver, and kidneys of animals like cows and chickens, provide an excellent source of B vitamins, especially B12, B6, riboflavin, and folate, all critical for stress control. These B vitamins are important for the production of neurotransmitters like dopamine and serotonin, which help regulate mood and could reduce stress.

Blueberries offer health benefits including improved mood. High in flavonoid antioxidants, they possess powerful anti-inflammatory and neuroprotective effects and may help reduce stress-related inflammation and protect against stress-related cellular damage. Eating flavonoid-rich foods like blueberries may safeguard against depression and boost your mood.

Artichokes are delicious and rich sources of fibre and especially rich in gut-friendly prebiotics. Artichokes are also high in potassium, magnesium, and vitamins C and K, all of which are essential for a healthy stress response.

Eating whole, nutrient-rich carbohydrate sources like sweet potatoes may help lower levels of the stress hormone cortisol. Sweet potatoes are a whole food packed with nutrients that are important for stress response, such as vitamin C and potassium.[63]

Food high in vitamin B (particularly B12), like fortified whole grains and some animal sources, can help with the metabolism of cortisol, e.g., beef, chicken, eggs, fortified cereal, and organ meats.

Food high in omega-3 fatty acids can reduce inflammation. These include fatty fish, anchovies, avocados, chia seeds, flax seeds, herring, olive oil, salmon, sardines, tuna, and walnuts.

Magnesium-rich foods reduce inflammation, metabolize cortisol, and promote general relaxation. Sources include avocados, bananas, broccoli, dark chocolate, pumpkin seeds, and spinach.

Protein-rich foods promote balanced sugar levels. Chicken, turkey, fish, poultry, beans and legumes, almonds, eggs, lentils, lean beef, peanuts, quinoa, tuna, salmon, and shrimp are good options.

---

[63] www.healthline.com/nutrition/stress-relieving-foods

Gut-healthy foods like probiotic-rich and fermented foods can help balance blood sugar and reduce cholesterol. Greek yoghurt, kefir, kimchi, and sauerkraut are popular options.

By contrast, some foods raise cortisol levels and should be avoided. These include: alcohol, caffeine, high-sugar foods, simple carbohydrates such as cakes and pastries, and the liquid accompaniment to rough days, soda.

NATURE NURTURES

Nature offers us bounty and a pharmacy from its seeds, herbs, and sunshine. There are vitamins and minerals we can enjoy that taste good and leave us feeling good. Many chemical prescription medications create addiction and have serious side effects. It also takes a while for an individual to find the exact dosage, and the trial and error can play havoc on their minds, bodies, and relationships. It is helpful to seek the advice of a homeopath and nutritionist as you embrace holistic and sustainable solutions.

Valerian root: a plant native to Europe and Asia. For many centuries, people have used this root to help treat sleep problems, anxiety, and depression. It can be found in the form of tea, tablet, or tincture. More studies are underway, but valerian is generally safe. It may induce drowsiness, so taking it with alcohol or sedatives will add to this effect and could be dangerous. Naturally, any form of supplements, even herbal ones, should be discussed with a doctor.

Lavender: a flowering plant related to the mint family, popular for its fragrance. It has been used to help calm the nerves and alleviate anxiety. It can be used in tea and its oil in aromatherapy, as massage or bath oil, or made into a spray for rooms and pillows. Lavender essential oil contains chemicals called terpenes. A 2017 study suggests that two of these terpenes, called linalool and linalyl acetate, may have a calming effect on chemical receptors in the brain.[64]

Passionflower: may be effective in treating restlessness, nervousness, and anxiety. According to a 2010 review of complementary treatments, some evidence suggests that the anti-anxiety effects compare favourably to those of benzodiazepines, which doctors typically prescribe for anxiety.

Kava kava: a shrub native to the islands of the Pacific Ocean, where inhabitants use it in a ceremonial beverage intended to relieve stress and alter mood.

Cannabidiol (CBD): one of the active ingredients of the hemp plant. 2019 research suggests that CBD may

---

[64] www.medicalnewstoday.com/articles/herbs-for-anxiety#summary

have a calming effect on the central nervous system. It is used as tablets, oils, and creams and has also been known to calm epileptic patients when fitting with the use of the drug epidyolex, per epilepsy.org.uk.

Magnesium: using magnesium, in combination with herbs such as kava kava and St. John's Wort, may help to alleviate anxiety.

Essential fatty acids: may reduce stress in females who are premenstrual, pregnant, or menopausal.

High-dose sustained-release vitamin C: Females consuming this supplement may experience reduced anxiety and a less prominent increase in blood pressure in response to stress.

In general, herbal and homoeopathic remedies take longer to take effect than over-the-counter medications, but for the most part have fewer or less severe side effects. An herbalist or healthcare professional should provide guidance on viability, dosage, and duration as, here again, fine print and manufacturer disclaimers can be an issue.

When it comes to holistic wellbeing, it is best to find nourishment and activity that preclude the use (and potential addiction and reliance) on medication and supplements. Recognise and manage triggers, and work towards fulfilment rather than fads and quick fixes

Vitality Tips

- ➤ *Invest in what truly matters today, three days, or five years from now. Don't let others and society lure you into mental and spiritual places that deplete your resources and cause undue stress.*

- ➤ *Eat for wellness.*

- ➤ *Infuse joy and gratitude into all you do; modern society punts work and material accomplishment.*

- ➤ *Be mindful about what your waking thoughts are.*

- ➤ *Work at assertiveness, and unapologetically walk away from people and situations that detract from your purpose*

CHAPTER SEVEN

FOOD AND HEALING

We are created with an amazing body that can heal itself, if we look after it properly; this is an existential and spiritual responsibility. There may come a time when the damage is too far gone for reparation work, and with a pressured world filled with processed everything, prevention is better than cure—as long as we give the body what it needs to do its work.

Our health and wellbeing journey requires many steps and many daily decisions and is largely influenced by factors such as our genetics, personal vision, values, resources, and priorities. Above all, it requires personal accountability. Our health and vitality are things we will need all our life, but, regrettably, we often take them for granted as we go from one task or goal to another. We can change this by making good decisions before we receive a scary diagnosis, ultimatum, or one of those restrictive diets that sap the joy out of life.

YOU CAN'T OUTSOURCE YOUR HEALTH

With all the advancements and innovations, shortcuts often look quite alluring, and there are also excellent medical and alternative healing options, but our relationship with them is just that: a relationship. And as we know, all relationships demand commitment and work. This means we need to follow advice and test solutions rather than jump from one treatment regime to another, or do only the parts we enjoy and ignore the rest. It has to be a relationship that works, so find a healthcare professional who helps you on your journey of health, as it will require time, energy, and effort.

It is important for us to be honest and upfront, to build trust, and avoid a co-dependent relationship. Some lifestyle diseases can be overcome completely, necessitating no over-the-counter or prescription medication, through committed, holistic lifestyle and diet changes. The other side of that coin is the possibility of being disease-free but following an unhealthy lifestyle, like long nights, substance abuse, and toxic relationships that can, in time, precipitate illness. A fast-paced lifestyle easily normalises unhealthy weights, renders smoking and drinking fashionable, and sees burnout and overwork as badges of honour and accomplishment.

Taking personal accountability for our physical and mental health comes down to self-care, committing to adequate nutrition and activity, and avoiding risky behaviour. Finding out information about diet and recipes, exercise regimes, and stress management techniques is one step; only acting on that information, however, will deliver desired changes. There can be no denial and no excuses. No one is pouring bad food and alcohol down our throats, and sometimes we have to engage enormous amounts of willpower to choose good nutrients over takeout.

We will have to use our drive, personality, and long-term goals to find our unique strategy for maintaining health. For some of us, it may be a food journal, monthly reward, or a non-judgmental accountability partner. Very few things beat the feeling of wellbeing and fitness and seeing our children enjoying their sports and hobbies because they're fuelling up on the good stuff. Good health gives us the energy to achieve goals and develop confidence in other life dimensions.

Like using eye cream before you develop wrinkles, prevention is the key to longevity. It doesn't have to be a life of restriction and suffering, either; there are thousands of healthy recipes that make sustainable health a delicious daily dose of creativity and passion. Human beings don't like change, and the uphill of anything feels too much like sacrifice, so, when our good eating habits become a way of life, it's easier when obstacles and curveballs and stressors come our way.

It may require that we prioritise check-ups, goals, and health milestones as we organise the rest of our lives. That's what our devices and tracking apps are for; there are tools and techniques for every health goal. We simply need to stick with it.

When our health is a means rather than an end in itself, a vehicle rather than a destination, we can keep reworking our game plan with our eye on the big prize (purpose and contribution). When we want to be fit to complete a marathon in support of destitute families, climb Mt. Everest, or have an easy pregnancy, we are more likely to stick with commitments grounded in our values.

TIPS TO STICK WITH PERSONAL HEALTH GOALS

* Love and treasure your body (don't condemn and criticize yourself)
* Understand how your brain and body work
* Know your food and drink intimately
* Know your *Why*; meditate on and reaffirm your purpose
* Visualise yourself well enough to achieve your goals
* Devise your Personal Wellness Plan
* Understand and manage your triggers
* Plan for setbacks and have a Plan B

* Set clear, exciting, and manageable goals

* Track your progress; what gets measured gets treasured

* Surround yourself with like-minded people

* Share your holistic lifestyle journey; you can be a huge source of inspiration for others (cue YouTube)

* Celebrate the successes and reward yourself

* Get healthy while enjoying yourself; find methods that resonate with your overall life and integrate your steps seamlessly

* Laugh, run, roll; embrace your inner child and the rest becomes easy

* Do a social clean-up; rid yourself of negative influences, whether on your social media feed, at your doorstep, or in your head

* Get enough quality rest

* Seek help. At times we may require professional help; do what you need with your eye on the bigger picture

PERSONAL ASSESSMENT: KNOWING WHAT YOUR BODY NEEDS

It will tell you! No one size fits all...

Any journey into health and wellbeing starts by building an understanding of where you are in life and being mindful of your own needs. A self-assessment is very helpful. Most workplaces and insurance providers make interim health assessments mandatory, and they partner with wellness and fitness providers to incentivise healthier living.

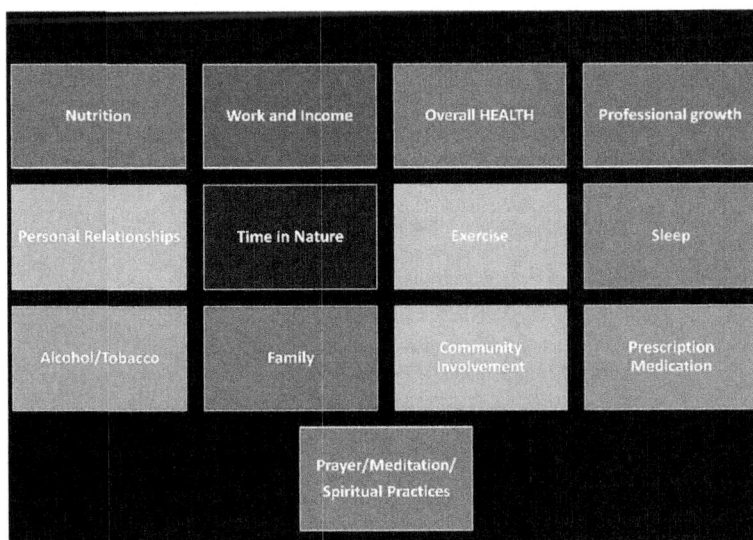

Nutrition	Work and Income	Overall HEALTH	Professional growth
Personal Relationships	Time in Nature	Exercise	Sleep
Alcohol/Tobacco	Family	Community Involvement	Prescription Medication
	Prayer/Meditation/ Spiritual Practices		

We need a baseline from which to work, so listening to the cues are critical. Clarity is needed to stay focused and in control of a well-balanced life.

SYSTEMIC SELF-ASSESSMENT TOOL

A. Consider the elements in the diagram above over a thirty-day period. Note your comfort level in each on a scale of 1 to 3, with 1 being *Not Comfortable*, 2 being *Not Sure*, and 3 being *Very Comfortable*:

B. Answer all of the following questions:

- Clearly state what is working in your overall profile.
- Clearly list what isn't working.
- Where do you evidence the problems?
- Is it a short-term reality or is it a recurring pattern?
- What causes it?

C. Make notes about what has to change.

- Which changes are within your control?
- How willing are you to live a better life?
- What is currently preventing your from making small changes?
- Where will you start?
- Who will support you?

I find that the magic is in the detail, so when I want to make impactful changes, I hone in on one particular category and break it down to granular units and build my action plan from there.

Example: Getting Granular with my Nutrition

Over a 30-day period, I consider my decisions and behaviour around:

- ✓ Monthly menu: vegetables, fruit, meat, grains, dairy
- ✓ Monthly events: dinners, parties, client meetings, travel (how do they impact what I eat and drink)
- ✓ Monthly shopping list
- ✓ Meal preparation
- ✓ Meal replacements and supplements (where applicable)
- ✓ Cooked meals vs takeaways/junk food
- ✓ 3 set meals or snacking or 5 smaller daily meals
- ✓ Gut health in relation to eating patterns: bloating, diarrhea, constipation, healthy bowel movements, nausea, vomiting
- ✓ Energy levels: am I eating well enough to have the energy I need for exercise, playing with and support the children, and doing community work?
- ✓ What 1% daily improvement can I make to my diet?

Example: Getting Granular about Stress

I generally don't suffer with distress as much as I used to, but lifelong maintenance is the investment I consciously make. The following self-reflections guide me:

- What's happening with my health, finances, work, personal life, spiritual life and community responsibility? The most important question is always: Am I still doing the right things?

- What is working well?

- What is causing me distress?

- Do I have an accurate perspective on it? What else could be true in this case?

- How do I feel about my communication in various settings? How well am I staying in the present and not allowing my past to negatively impact my here and now?

- What important events are happening this week/month? This applies to my schedule as well as the family's.

- What can I do by way of preparation?

- Do I have/need a Plan B?

- Which tasks can be shared / delegated?

- How many hours have I spent relaxing?

- Which soul-feeding activities have I engaged in, i.e., quality time with the family, cooking, experimenting with new recipes, learning something new of interest?

MEDITATION, WORSHIP, AND PRAYER

These are some ideas to get your Personal Wellness Plan started. Focus on the areas where you want the greatest traction, or where you could achieve better integration.

We can effectively self-regulate and let our bodies tell us what it needs, whether it be sleep, physical activity, water, exercise, sunlight, company, greater stimulation, or a break.

Increase your conscious awareness to name the sensation or emotion you are feeling, and learn to make connections between and among the various aspects of your life. This is best way to identify and resolve systemic issues. From this wellbeing and vitality will follow.

Slow down. Pencil in the time, if you need to. And learn to recognize what our mind and body require. This will help provide clarity and motivation to make positive, permanent changes.

ALLERGIES

Allergies are physical conditions in which the immune system overreacts to certain substances that are triggering an allergic reaction. The immune system targets and protects us against threats like viruses and harmful bacteria.

The most common allergies include foods, animals, pollen, different types of mould, dust mites, medications, insect bites, cockroaches, and perfumes or household chemicals. Even soap, face cream, fabric softeners, and commercial air fresheners can send our bodies into distress.

Once an allergen enters your body, your immune system reacts and starts to make antibodies. Antibodies can be so specific that they only target certain types of pollen or mould, for example. When the immune system detects an allergen, more of the proper antibodies are produced, and these start to search for the offending allergen and eventually destroy it.

When antibodies recognise an allergen, they start to alert mast cells, which are blood cells that release more chemicals, including histamine. Histamine, in turn, causes inflammation, and our tiny blood vessels become leaky. As the fluid escapes, this leads to symptoms such as a runny nose, nasal swelling, or congestion.

While some allergic reactions are mild and restricted, to certain parts of the body, anaphylaxis is severe and affects the health of the whole body. It comes on quickly, and it can be deadly. It causes tissues to release histamine along with other substances that cause breathing problems and other symptoms, like abdominal pain, dizziness, difficulty swallowing, facial swelling, and unconsciousness.

FOOD ALLERGIES

It's not uncommon to occasionally have a bad reaction to foods, such as headaches from drinking wine or coughing from spicy food. Lactose intolerance could trigger diarrhoea when consuming dairy. These food sensitivities or intolerances are different from allergies in that they are not immune-system reactions. With a food allergy, the immune system reacts to specific foods, which can result in symptoms that range from mild skin rashes or itching to anaphylaxis, which can be fatal.

When the body has an immune system reaction to a specific food, it produces antibodies to that food. These symptoms may occur immediately after eating the specific food, or hours later. Food allergy symptoms may include:

- ✓ Skin rash
- ✓ Hives
- ✓ Swelling of the tongue or throat
- ✓ Breathing problems including asthma
- ✓ Vomiting or diarrhea
- ✓ Stomach pain

In severe cases, the allergic reaction may trigger a drop in blood pressure, unconsciousness, or death.

Common food allergens include:

- ✓ Milk (mostly in children)
- ✓ Eggs
- ✓ Peanuts and Tree nuts (e.g., walnuts and hazelnuts)
- ✓ Soy
- ✓ Wheat
- ✓ Fish and shellfish (mostly in adults)

FOOD INTOLERANCE

Food intolerance does not involve a reaction of the immune system.[65] For instance, lactose intolerance is a common food intolerance. The lactose intolerant lack the enzyme (lactase) needed to digest sugar found in dairy, called lactose. This condition results in gas, bloating, and abdominal pain. It can be treated with lactase tablets that help people to digest dairy.

There are also a wide range of lactose-free dairy products on the market. Check for contraindications, and keep a food diary, noting down foods and symptoms. Food intolerances and food allergies are managed differently.

A milk allergy is different from lactose intolerance. Being allergic means a negative a reaction to milk

---

[65] www.mayoclinic.org/diseases-conditions/food-allergy/symptoms-causes/syc-20355095

proteins such as casein. Some people cannot ingest cow's milk, but they are able to keep down goat's milk. Others cannot have any type of milk at all.

Symptoms of a milk allergy include stomach pain, diarrhoea, hives, or difficulty breathing. With lactose intolerance, there may be bloating or gas but no allergic reaction symptoms.

The only way to prevent an allergic reaction to a food is to avoid that food. Eating out or receiving food is risky, if you have an allergy; you'll have to be extra-careful, because you don't know what's happening in other kitchens, pantries, or on other cutting boards and draining racks. Read labels and fine print carefully. Apart from milk, ingredients such as casein or whey which are components of dairy milk also pose a risk. The problem with processed food is that it often contains products you don't expect or associate with the main one such as instant cereals, baked goods and packet mashed potatoes all contain milk.

PEANUT ALLERGY

Peanuts are a common food allergen with fairly severe reactions. In some cases, the reaction is so severe that people can go into fatal anaphylaxis.

Peanuts are used in a wide variety of foods, flavourings, sauces, marinades, thickeners, snack foods, confectionery, oils, and sweets. African, Chinese, Malay,

Indian, Mexican, Thai, and Vietnamese cuisine often contain peanuts. It can be delicious and deadly, if you're severely allergic, so err on the side of caution and find suitable alternatives.

WHEAT ALLERGY

Similarly common, an allergic reaction to wheat is actually an intolerance to gluten, a protein found in grains such as wheat, rye, and barley. Gluten intolerance is associated with "gluten-sensitive enteropathy," more commonly known as celiac disease. Symptoms of celiac disease include gas, bloating, diarrhoea, weight loss, fatigue, and sometimes vomiting. Even gluten-free bread may contain small amounts of wheat from its bakery or processing facility.

Wheat is also present in ale, beer, bourbon, and whiskey; wine is generally considered gluten-free and safe for celiacs or the intolerant. A few medications in tablet form have a starch binder not listed on the label, though that is potato or corn starch, not wheat starch (which doesn't contain much if any gluten, anyway). While the United States FDA is aware of no oral drug products currently marketed in the United States that contain wheat gluten or wheat flour intentionally added as an inactive ingredient, you can seek out a liquid form of medication, if you are concerned.

Food allergy symptoms usually develop within a few minutes to two hours after eating the offending food. The most common food allergy signs and symptoms include:

- ✓ Tingling or itchy mouth
- ✓ Hives, itching or eczema on the skin
- ✓ Swelling of the lips, face, tongue, throat, or other body parts
- ✓ Wheezing, nasal congestion, or difficulty breathing
- ✓ Abdominal pain, diarrhea, nausea, or vomiting
- ✓ Dizziness, light-headedness or fainting[66]

In some people, a food allergy can trigger anaphylaxis. This can cause life-threatening signs and symptoms, including:

- ✓ Constriction and tightening of the airways
- ✓ A swollen throat or the sensation of a lump in your throat, hampering normal breathing
- ✓ Shock with a severe drop in blood pressure
- ✓ Racing pulse

---

[66] www.mayoclinic.org/diseases-conditions/food-allergy/symptoms-causes/syc-20355095

✓ Dizziness, light-headedness, or loss of consciousness

Emergency treatment is critical for anaphylaxis. Left untreated, it can lead to coma or even death.

RECOGNISING YOUR ALLERGY TRIGGERS

It's very easy to come in contact with allergens, because they're everywhere, airborne, both inside and outdoors. Playing with a pet, sweeping and dusting, or taking a walk during certain seasons can set off your allergies.

Medications are designed to treat a particular condition but may trigger another one. For example, anti-inflammatory pills have been known to cause gastric problems including nausea and diarrhoea. Antibiotics are often prescribed with probiotics/plain yoghurt, because they wreak havoc on the gut. An allergic reaction to penicillin can cause death.

There is an increase in marketing of medication, ointments, and elixirs, vitamins, and foods containing vitamins and minerals. It all looks very enticing, with the subtext that they will fix everyone's ailments. Supermarkets also have medication and in-house pharmacies with specials on painkillers and all the rest. It's easy to be tempted into trying these concoctions as we would a pair of shoes or a magazine. Or to share medication amongst our family or social groups. But there are no guarantees.

Due to our physical and environmental constitution, we may develop temporary or lifelong allergies to certain foods, as well. The consequences of food allergies range from mild to fatal, thus it is critical to note any reactions and changes immediately. Reading ingredient labels and avoiding some food groups completely may be the safest way to figure out how to plan and prepare nutritious meals and snacks. Even cross-contamination through using a utensil or cutting board containing the allergen can bring dire results. When your little children battle allergies, it is important to inform their schools, sports teams and peer groups to be on the safe side.

ALLERGY TREATMENTS

Abstinence is the first and best defence. Thereafter, a number of medications are available.

- ✓ Antihistamines: ease itching, sneezing, runny nose, and the hives often caused by seasonal and indoor allergies
- ✓ Decongestants: reduce nasal congestion
- ✓ Nasal sprays
- ✓ Corticosteroid creams or ointments: relieve itching and rashes
- ✓ Oral corticosteroids: reduce swelling and treat severe allergic reactions

✓ Epinephrine: treats life-threatening reactions like anaphylaxis

✓ Allergy injections

VARIETY AND THE SPICE OF LIFE: RETHINKING BALANCE

We decide what balance means in our lives, because it cannot be overlaid over someone else's. That means you have an opportunity, but also a responsibility, when it comes to life balance. You can't look to your boss, friends, gurus, or celebrities to define it for you... If you leave it up to academia, you could easily lose your balance, wading through more than 230 different conceptualizations of balance in the academic research: e.g., work-life balance, work-family balance, work-family conflict, work/non-work balance, and so on. There are of course common themes, but the point is the decision and action rests with you.

The goal is to create some level of integration among your life dimensions. Your life doesn't have to mimic anyone else's, but that in itself can create pressure on yourself and your relationships. You will know best what a meaningful life of happiness, joy, and service looks like. From my perspective, I found that my improved health gave met Energy, Motivation, and the Mental Space to be more and do more.

I want a Blessed Life with some degree of balance (mostly from my diet).

It's about quantity and quality: how much time you invest in various areas of your life; but also, whether or not you are fully present during that time. I love work, and my children's needs were always primary in my deciding where I work. But I also need energy to study and volunteer and research and experiment. I eat to live, to get around all the key roles in my life.

I strive constantly to improve myself, because this serves as a living example to my children. I take my job as a role model very seriously, and together, we can keep growing as individuals and as a family. Having endured years of hardship and emotional trauma, I learned to eke out the goodness in the moments I go through. The 90% of my life experience comes from the quality and accuracy of my perceptions, many of which I've had to reevaluate over the years. That's growing up and the rich maturity of embracing new levels.

One of our biggest challenges in modern living is sifting through all the things we could do and settling on the ones that truly matter. We can often overcomplicate things in our pursuit of what is advertised as "the good life." When we immerse ourselves in meaningful tasks, it's about the time we allocate to it but also our ability to be fully present. Sometimes, we can make it to the event and not emotionally and spiritually show up; this means we may have to consider the other elements of our life and make readjustments.

One of the reasons people are so stressed out these days, particularly in the workplace, is that long work hours and juggling hordes of personal and professional responsibilities don't often enough translate into feelings of competence and joy. Our activities must align to our purpose, values, and goals. Everything else is peripheral.

It doesn't have to be equal across all domains. Decide which areas need more attention at different times. Be clear to yourself and others about your priorities and values. Priorities are fluid, but the vision remains constant: who you want to be and what you want to bring should persist.

The natural order of sequences and cycles give us the seasons, and within those are endless variety, change, and inconsistency. Just as nature seeks to balance itself with change, so, too, do our bodies need that balance.[67] Finding balance is a lifetime endeavour and will need reworking throughout the rhythms of our life stages, without force or haste.

---

[67] www.gomacro.com/elements-of-a-balanced-life/.

BALANCE IS ALSO ABOUT STRESS MANAGEMENT

By the time we can articulate that we want or need more balance, it is probably desperate roundabout speak and a niggly desire for "less stress." It could be your immune system punctuating the sentences on your To Do list and your Ways to Escape Social Gatherings list.

Distress or overwhelming levels of physical and mental stress holds us in survival mode, where our responses to the outside world are limited to three: fight, flight, or freeze. Fun, meaningful impact, joy, and bliss do not operate at that level.

Maintaining some form of balance means using positive stress to our benefit and to navigate negative stressors. Life happens, and our batteries run down. That's how we learn and gain a deeper understanding of what it means to be human, to fail, to succeed, to love, and grow. Besides, if everything stood still, we would cease to exist. We're going to need a healthy body and a healthy mind, and they are interdependent. It's not about avoidance; it's the Courage and the Comeback that are the real game changer.

Boosting your happiness rebuilds energy, motivation, and creativity. It is well known that the most resilient and confident people effectively use humour and can laugh at themselves. There's no use taking life too seriously, especially if you have your sights set on changing that life. Science tells us laughter is great for alleviating stress and fortifying our bodies against infections, boosting our brains, and lowering blood pressure. And, of course, it gives us rosier outlook on situations.[68]

VARIETY AND FOOD

Nutrition is more than just eating the right things to give us energy throughout the day, and small changes can create lasting positive results and bring control back to a busy life. It's not about the obsession to be a certain weight, but more about having the energy and headspace to do the things that matter. Our daily decisions and habits build our character, and thus we feed ourselves and our wellbeing one spoon or forkful at a time.

Healthy eating provides balance, achieved through variety and moderation. Too much of anything is bad, so know your nutrients, and create the enjoyable equilibrium on your plate.

Make sure to eat a variety of nutrient-rich foods. You need more than forty different nutrients for good health, and no single food supplies them all. Your daily food selection should include vegetables, fruits, bread,

---

[68] www.everydayhealth.com/healthy-living/how-to-live-a-well-balanced-life.aspx.

dairy products, meat and poultry, fish, other protein foods, and whole grain products.

A healthy weight depends on your age, sex, height, genetics, and activity levels. The goal is to prevent lifestyle diseases, so a balanced diet and exercise are important.

VITALITY TIPS

> *Wellness and Happiness are parts of an Inside Job; you can't outsource or postpone optimal health.*

> *Add Personal Wellness to your priorities (if not already done).*

> *Your diet will largely influence your energy and motivation levels. How will you ensure that you're eating and drinking for vitality?*

> *Seek professional advice for persistent conditions, and always ask for a nutritionist's perspective on medication. (Chances are, if you're eating well and avoiding inflammatory foods, your immune system will already be stronger.)*

> *Check allergic reactions to food, environment, and lifestyle changes. Moving to a new climate or geography may trigger some physiological changes. Allergies can be treated; you don't have to suffer. Read the labels and fine-print diligently.*

> *Find you own brand of balance by reaffirming your values and priorities. Use a three-, six-, or twelve-*

month view, and conduct weekly reflections to align activities and investments to the plan. Identify enablers and detractors. Take decisive action, and celebrate your progress

➢ *Create and revisit your Personal Wellness Goals at least twice a year (more frequently if you're treating a specific condition).*

CHAPTER EIGHT

GUT HEALTH

2500 years ago, the father of modern science made a statement that changed the face of medical research: "All diseases begin in the gut." In 400 B.C, Hippocrates proposed a theory that faced the trial of time, and while all diseases do not literally begin the gut, research has proven how autoimmune, cognitive, and metabolic disturbances indeed rise from an unhealthy gut. Thousands of years later, research now strongly emphasises the importance of a healthy gut for optimal health and overall wellbeing.

Gut health is the state of your digestive tract. Over the last several years, the term "gut health" has earned more prominence as research studies attempt to identify the components of a healthy gut and how it influences the overall wellbeing of a person.

Gut health is often referred to as the balance and function of the bacteria in the gastrointestinal tract, also known as the gut microbiome. The intestines, stomach, and oesophagus work together to digest the food ingested with ease and without discomfort. However, research suggests otherwise for the four-tenths of people in the world suffering from gastrointestinal disorders.

The human gastrointestinal microbiome hosts trillions of fungi, bacteria, Archaea, viruses, and other organisms responsible for the neurotransmission, immunity, metabolism, and contribution to homeostatic regulation of energy and food. These trillions of organisms in our gut make it a very complex ecosystem to understand.

THE ROLE OF THE MICROBIOME IN GUT HEALTH

Scientists regard the gut microbiome as one of the most important medical research discoveries in recent decades. It is often quoted as "an organ bigger than the liver." And regardless of how much the Internet says it knows about how a microbiome works, scientists are still discovering how various foods interact with a gut microbiome.

But from what they have discovered, the gut microbiome is responsible for the absorption of nutrients, aiding digestion, regulating the body's processes such as vitamin levels, and providing adequate energy to the immune system.

Larger than the average human brain, the two-kilogram gut microbiome contains almost twice as many genes as the human genome. While there are microbes everywhere in the body, from our mouth to skin and lungs, the gut microbiome is the largest in the body and has the most impact on our short-term to long-term health. The organisms found in the gut microbiome vary from person to person, making it extremely complex to study. According to recent research by European Bioinformatics Institute in 2020, there are more than 2,000 species found in gut microbes previously unknown and not yet been cultured in the lab.

As scientists research its importance to bodily functions, they have determined that imbalances in gut bacteria are a leading cause of chronic diseases such as diabetes, IBS, and carcinoma. Research also finds a massive link between depression, autoimmune diseases, and cholesterol levels to gut health.

Gut microbes are responsible for things that the gut cannot perform, such as synthesising and liberating nutrients from the food we eat, producing metabolites, developing short-chain fatty acids for immunity, metabolising glucose, and moderating inflammatory responses. A gut microbiome requires up to 30g of fiber every day to efficiently perform these tasks. The average take of fibre of people around the globe is 9-20g a day.

And that is just one example of what is contributing to the growing health concerns across the globe.

How Gut Health Affects the Body

For millions of years, microbes have evolved with humans. The gut microbiome starts working the moment you are born. The first interaction of a human being with microbes is during birth, and they begin to diversify as you grow. Lower microbiome diversity in the gut indicates poor gut health, whereas a higher microbiome results from the nutrient-rich gut.

The food we eat has a massive impact on the gut bacteria that affects our overall health in several ways. A few examples of how gut performs are:

Digesting Breast Milk

At birth, gut bacteria are activated and multiply to digest and synthesise healthy sugars from breast milk. The gut bacteria inside a newborn baby are known as *Bifidobacteria*.

Controls Immune System

Gut health directly affects the immune system. How a person's immune system performs is greatly dependent on the health of the gut to communicate immune cells. A gut microbiome controls the way your body responds to infection.

Monitors brain health

The gut microbiome and its health influence the central nervous system, as well. The central nervous system is responsible for conducting brain function, emphasising the importance of the gut-brain connection.

These are just a few of the many ways in which the gut microbiome regulates and affects the bodily function of a person.

Understanding Gut Dysbiosis

It was previously assumed that gut health only impacted digestion, but scientists have recently discovered and emphasised the importance of a healthy gut microbiome for overall wellbeing. Disturbances in gut microbes can cause gut dysbiosis.

Our body hosts thousands of harmless bacteria called microbiota. Mostly, many colonies of bacteria positively affect our body and contribute to supporting the body's natural processes. Imbalances in bacterial colonies lead to gut dysbiosis. In mild cases, gut dysbiosis is associated with indigestion or an upset stomach. However, serious indications include obesity and inflammation.

Think of the gut microbiome as a balanced ecosystem threatened by our food choices. The imbalance in the ecosystem of our gut microbiome results in various diseases, including mental illness, obesity, gastrointestinal disorders, and more.

Several factors are responsible for throwing off the balance of the ecosystem of our gastrointestinal tract, including physical stress, dietary changes, hygiene, antibiotic use, sleep, radiation, and altered peristalsis.

THE GUT-BRAIN CONNECTION

Throughout history, we have known about the strong association between the gut and the brain. "Butterflies in the stomach," "Gut-wrenching experience," "Trust your gut" are not coincidental terms but scientific facts that have confirmed the link between the gut and the human nervous system.

Regarded as the "second brain," there is a lining of more than 100 million nerves on the GI tract, composed of actually the same tissues as the central nervous system. In fact, scientists argue that the profoundly interconnected gut and brain are not two but one system. While the gut cannot memorise or write a novel, it can arrange and trigger hormones, neurotransmitters, and electrical impulses.

Nutrition plays a significant role in the functioning and development of the brain. The effects of nutritional mechanisms are widely studied, and they impact almost all aspects of neurological functions, including neural pathways, neurogenesis, neurotrophic factors, and neuroplasticity. Therefore, gut health interplays closely with neurological functioning.

Mounting evidence reveals the importance of a healthy gut for the central nervous system. The brain/gut relationship is also called the "gut-brain axis," which covers neural, endocrine, and immune pathways. Medical research is now exploring the "gut-brain axis" to address a range of mental health conditions, including anxiety, depression, and its association with GI disorders such as diarrhoea or constipation.

FOOD AS A MEDICINE

The microbiome differs from person to person and is constantly evolving according to the lifestyle of its host. The health of the gut microbiome can be improved and maintained by increasing the percentage of "good" bacteria in the body. There are various ways to do that, but the most powerful and easiest is simply by manipulating the diet.

The food we eat is the most important determinant of the composition of the microbiota. The gut microbiome responds the fastest to healthy food choices, proving that Hippocrates was somewhat correct in arguing that "all diseases begin in the gut."

PROBIOTICS, PREBIOTICS, AND THE GOOD BACTERIA

Certain foods have been identified as the most beneficial for promoting and maintaining a healthy gut microbiome. These foods are categorised as probiotic and prebiotic foods. Prebiotics stimulate the growth of good bacteria in the colon and improve both digestion and the host's overall health.

Plant-based, high-fibre foods are a great source of prebiotics. Certain foods that have been medically shown to increase the good bacteria through prebiotics in the colon and to improve gut microbiome include garlic, oatmeal, chicory root, artichokes, asparagus, leeks, beans, and vegetables.

Prebiotics are nondigestible components of food, while probiotics are live microorganisms found in fermented food items such as yoghurt, apple cider vinegar, cheese, kombucha, etc. Bacteria and other microorganisms found in probiotics digest food, produce vitamins, and destroy cells that cause diseases. Many microorganisms found in probiotics are the same as microorganisms naturally found in our bodies.

While probiotics have widespread benefits, there is no standard diet or food for practice. There are hundreds of different types of bacteria found under the hood of probiotics, each having unique functions and benefits for the body.

One of the most widely researched families of probiotics includes Bifidobacterium, Lactobacillus, Streptococcus, and different yeast varieties. Different strains of Lactobacillus probiotics have been proven to improve gut health and bodily functions, including diarrhoea, improving depression and anxiety, boosting immunity, reducing infection and inflammation, maintaining neurological health, vaginal conditions, and inhibiting dental caries. Similarly, Bifidobacterium reduces inflammation by stimulating immune cells, improving the symptoms of depression, and reducing clinical inflammation and eczema in infants. Found in yeast, Saccharomyces boulardii is an effective probiotic that has been recognised to treat various GI conditions, including diarrhoea and difficile infection.

DIETARY FIBRES

Plant-based soluble and insoluble dietary fibres feed gut microbiota and eliminate the risk of chronic diseases. Dietary fibres have fermentation and viscose properties that improve digestion and prevent disease. Other compounds in dietary fibres, such as flavonoids, have the ability to modulate the gut microbiome.

Chronic diseases including cancer, diabetes, cardiovascular disease, and inflammation can be prevented by maintaining a high-fibre diet. People who consume fibre-rich diets have been shown in population studies to be less vulnerable to chronic disease.

Fibre-rich prebiotics have anti-inflammatory and antioxidant properties such as minerals, vitamins, and phytonutrients that fight diseases and provide various health benefits.

LIFESTYLE MEDICINE FOR A HEALTHY GUT

The purpose of eating is to enrich the body with vital nutrients necessary to maintain healthy bodily functions. While enjoying food is an integral part of human health, its primary concern is to aid bodily functions, provide nutrients for growth and repair, and regulate neurological systems. Eating to fuel the gut microbiome is essential to ensure wellbeing.

Over the years, humans have associated emotions with food. We eat when we are happy or sad. We eat to celebrate or out of mere boredom. As humans, we seem to have forgotten the actual purpose of food in our life.

When we realise that the purpose of food is good health, we automatically actualise it in the form of organic and minimally processed food choices. Processed foods, stripped of essential nutrients, do not serve any purpose, yet they add an additional burden on our body through fat, sugar, and salt. Eating food with its raw, naked essentials is what gives food its purpose and our body the nutrients to fight ailments and diseases, rather than hosting them in the form of highly cooked or processed food.

Lifestyle medicine is earning prominence as more and more research highlights the association of the gut microbiome with chronic diseases and psychological health. Lifestyle medicine practitioners are readily educating the world about the benefits of adopting a pathogen-free, healthy lifestyle based on an organic diet that has longstanding effects on the body's functions.

Fundamental steps in achieving a lifestyle that enriches the body and promotes holistic wellbeing of an individual include consuming a high fibre, probiotic-, and prebiotic-rich diet, getting proper sleep, engaging in physical activity, and practicing mindfulness.

The journey to holistic wellbeing is based on several aspects of life. While diet and food play a significant role in achieving the goal, other lifestyle changes such as mindfulness must be incorporated with eating habits in order to beat modern-day ailments, prevent diseases, and achieve a balanced gut-brain axis.

CHAPTER NINE

RESUSCITATION, REVERSAL AND RENEWAL

The health care industry widely recognises the connection between emotional and physical wellbeing. Stemming from the same narrative that discusses exercise as a means to reduce stress, new research now delves into previously overlooked topics such as mindfulness, sleep, and gut health. Positioned in the limelight of medical research, gut health remains the most widely studied topic to determine causes for mental and physical wellbeing.

Gut health affects not only physical but mental state, as well. And it becomes more believable when we ponder our everyday experiences, examining the interlinks between the two closely. How often do we experience anxiety when suffering from diarrhoea or constipation? Or feel nauseous, unable to eat, when feeling stressed?

For decades, medical science believed that depression and anxiety contributed to bowel problems; however, recent findings have discovered that gastrointestinal disorders are also responsible for emotional changes. They trigger anxiety and depression by sending signals to the central nervous system.

These findings form the basis of this chapter, which emphasizes the need to approach diet as a source of holistic wellbeing. Referred to as the "second brain" in holistic medicine, the gut-brain connection is dissected to understand gut health's neurological, emotional, and immune system responses.

A Deeper Analysis of Gut-Brain Axis

The gut and the brain communicate in both directions. The digestive tract receives signals from the brain about moving food quickly through the tract, secreting digestive juices to break down and absorb nutrients and maintaining the levels of inflammation. Our parasympathetic and sympathetic nervous systems are responsible for sending these signals down to the digestive tract.

The enteric nervous system can independently control the gastrointestinal behaviour of the nervous system. The millions of cells attached to our gut lining communicate information about gut health to the brain, such as infections in the tract and bloating of insufficient blood flow in the tract. The constant communication between the gut and the brain forms the basis of both gut and brain health.

Historically, we have associated unhealthy eating with weight and digestive issues. But the academic realms are now touching mental distress and achieving wholeness and happiness through healthy eating habits.

The gut-brain axis is an interesting find that brings us back to believing in the connectedness of all things in the universe and how our body hosts an entire ecosystem of its own, the balance of which must be restored to achieve holistic wellbeing. The gut-brain axis forms the basis of both psychiatric care and intestinal flora. Caring for intestinal flora can relieve anxiety symptoms, while treating anxiety can directly regulate gastrointestinal disorders. It seems that the association between our emotional wellbeing and gut is more intrinsic than previously believed.

Understanding the pivotal role gut health plays in our holistic wellbeing can return us to making conscious efforts that help us attend to it. Over the years, the term "health-consciousness" has evolved and taken many different faces, but for the most part, it is identified as a holistic state in which the mind, body, and emotions are in perfect sync. A holistic approach to nutrition and health maintains a balance between lifestyle habits, consciousness, emotional state, and eating habits.

HOLISTIC WELLNESS: CONSCIOUSNESS RESTORED

The fast-paced world we live in today has had us accustomed to conveniences in everyday activities, including how and what we eat. It seems more convenient to unwrap a package or open a can than cut slices of fruit or fresh vegetables, when hungry. Holistic nutritionists argue that the "convenient approach" to food is not only damaging to your health but emotional wellbeing as well. The rise of diabetes, obesity, and gastrointestinal disorders is not coincidental in the age of processed fast food.

The famous quote by Martha Beck, "The way you do anything is the way you do everything," is perfectly relevant to how our mental state reiterates itself in our everyday activities, including how we eat. For example, it is common to have dinner while watching television or looking at your phone. And before you realise it, the meal is finished. But how many of your senses were involved in the process of eating? How did your food smell? How many calories did you take? How many times did you breathe in while chewing? How many times did you actually see what you are eating? So, what exactly did we miss out on while being consciously disconnected from our food?

Mindfulness.

Although much is written about the health benefits of mindful eating, little has been emphasised on mindfulness's lasting psychological and digestive effects when eating.

Mindful eating applies mindful metacognitive skills to our eating behaviour. It is maintaining respectful, consciousness, and keen attention while eating. Mindful eating practices provide psychological changes that alter the "fight or flight" psychophysiological mode to "rest and digest" through the parasympathetic nervous system. By building relaxing sensations in the body, our mind naturally sends input to the digestive tract that supports gastrointestinal physiology and aids in the absorption of nutrients and digestion of food.

YOUR BODY IS A TEMPLE

Thousands of different species of viruses, bacteria, fungi, and various other cellular organisms live inside our skin, mouth, and gastrointestinal tract. Our gut microbiome starts functioning the minute we pass through the birth canal and enter into this world. It prepares our body for the first drop of milk and takes over our wellbeing from this point forward.

Whether it is the gut microbiome or our central nervous system, our body constantly struggles for our wellbeing. It keeps the heart beating, remembers to breathe, and allows you to feel the pains and pleasures of life.

Consciously recognise and reflect on your able-body with gratitude for all that does it for. Our body is a temple, a spiritual centre whose balance must be restored through conscious efforts.

So, how do we treat our body like a shrine? Remove pathogens and toxins from your body while consciously attending to what we put inside your body. Pharmacologic antibiotics and pesticides damage the microbiome. Food irradiation, GMO, overcooking, microwaving, and over sterilisation are all processes that kill off the microbiome even before the food is served on the plate. We replace good food with processed flours and refined sugars, filling our minds with the world's problems, spiralling us towards pain, chronic diseases, and autoimmune disorders.

So, in pursuit of conscious health reform, what are the two key steps to get us started?

1. Consume productive fuel. The mind and body work together. While eliminating preservatives and processed foods is the step towards conscious eating, observing the state of your mind is also important. Monitor the type of media, music, and reading material your mind observes. Consciously choose what fuels your mind and body.

We have all heard the phrase, "We reap what we sow." What energies we consume has the same effect on our minds as food has on our bodies. The energy we consume and the energy we release is a concept far beyond food; it encompasses all aspects of human interactions with internal and external energies.

Let's take the case of a temple as a reference to our discussion. A temple is the place of worship where we practice purity. Through physical actions such as wearing clean clothes, keeping the place of worship clean, and removing footwear signs from the premises, we attempt to achieve a superficial purity. However, every person who enters a place of worship aims to attain internal purity through physical actions. Clean clothes do not remove the impurities of the mind, unless we consciously choose to change the course of our thoughts.

Would the prayer count if there is malice in the heart? Would the prayer count if the mind is oblivious to the said words? While we keep the temple (outward) clean, the value of the prayer is defined by what is inside.

The balance of the mind and body is similar to this sync between the physical and the internal state. Physical cleanliness (good food) alone cannot make the prayer count without consciousness and purity of the heart (mindfulness).

Consuming good food without consciousness cannot help us attain optimum health, and therefore, the mind and body must work together to achieve this equilibrium.

2. Pay attention to your body. Listen to your body. Our body responds to energies surrounding us and speaks to us through pain, pleasure, joy, and sadness. Our muscle memory records even the simplest actions through a complex process of tensing and relaxing different muscles that automatically perform over time. And even though our body adjusts to a wrong posture or too much sugar, it communicates to us what it actually needs. We often confuse cravings with what our body wants, while it is actually indicating dehydration or low blood sugar levels.

Take time to understand your body and consciously recognise the messages it communicates. For example, when we are conscious of the portion we eat, we will realise when our body is full. It is common to overeat after a long day or a big gap between meals. We assume that our body must require more portions, because we have starved ourselves for so long. However, that's not true.

When we eat consciously, our mind and body are in sync, allowing us to slow down and prevent us from reaching a point of desperation.

Mindful Eating: Create an Experience

A commonly used term now, *mindfulness*, has a more profound meaning than its everyday use in our multitasking and socially driven contexts. However, whatever the context, people use this term to urge consciousness to achieve health and goodness. Mindful eating refers to the conscious awareness of what goes inside our mouths.

By giving purposeful attention to our food, mindful eating is a method that focuses on sensual awareness of the experience of food. Unlike diet plans and weight-loss regimes, mindful eating has nothing to do with measuring protein, carbohydrates, and fat levels. It means to savour the moment, eat without judgment, and ensure perfect sync of your mind and body while eating. Mindful eating is also regarded as "complete presence."

Diet plans set the rules of eating, e.g., how much to eat and what to eat, with the intent to achieve certain outcomes—reducing or gaining weight, improving stamina, reducing cholesterol, etc. They are inflexible with no guarantee of success or failure. The outcomes highly depend on consumption, regularity, and the effectiveness of the plan. But it is rare not to experience results when practising mindfulness.

Mindfulness is not an outcome-driven plan; it is a process-oriented approach to life. For being present in the moment, experiencing every bite, and savouring the experience. In mindful eating, a person chooses what to eat and how much to eat. And, therefore, it is common for people eating mindfully to consume less, be selective, and achieve desirable results.

Mindful eating brings our attention to the food, wherever and whenever we eat. It makes us more aware of what we eat and alters our association with food by encouraging a more health-driven holistic perspective to eating. Ultimately, eating mindfully gives us a better chance to opt for foods that nourish us and help us stay healthy, while also appreciating every morsel and every ingredient on our plate.

ENGAGING SENSES

How often do we observe the food we are eating? When was the last time you were truly alone with your food? The world in which we live today works on autopilot. We eat our meals while being hooked to screens with little or no time to focus on our senses.

Mindfulness helps us eliminate these distractions and enjoy uninterrupted meals. We begin to slowly reconnect to our senses and become more aware of our experiences by engaging in mindful practices. The flavours, texture, and aroma combine to heighten our sensory experience and help us understand what our body communicates through meals, what ingredients suit us, and what ingredients cause us trouble. The flavours, the texture, and the aroma all combine

MINDFUL METHODS: CULTIVATION, REARING, AND PREPARATION

1. Ask

The first step to mindful eating is to ask ourselves the basic question:

A. *Why* am I eating? Is it to curb hunger, to satiate a craving, or merely out of boredom?

B. *What* am I eating? Is this food good? Would it nourish my body and my mind? Or simply make me feel full? Will by body regret this?

These two questions form the basis of the mindful eating practice. Understanding the purpose of eating is the first step to realise whether the food you eat will help or wreak havoc.

2. Chew Well

The process of digestion starts from the mouth. When we chew our food, the enzymes found in saliva help our body absorb the essential nutrients and liberate the benefits of the food in our body. Focus your attention on the process of chewing. See that you are not swallowing big chunks of food, as it inhibits digestion and leads to bloating.

3. Dine Gracefully

The act of dining is a form of meditation in itself. With the pace at which life is moving these days, most of us grab our meals on the go. Catching a sandwich on our way to work and drinking coffee while driving. The lack of a calm state when eating directly affects digestion.

Allow yourself to sit down and experience the meal with the utmost attention. Indulge in flavours, the aroma, and texture, instead of swallowing bite after bite.

4. Engage your mind

Whether you engage your breath or dine in a formal sitting to practice mindfulness, engaging your mind is the key to any kind of mindful practice.

Regulating thoughts and tuning in your mind to the moment is the most important aspect of mindful eating. It is common for our minds to wander. A hundred thoughts pass by our mind while eating that must be controlled, in order to be present with our food.

Being fully present in the moment helps us become more of every sensation in our body. These sensations become our guide to wellness.

5. Be grateful

Before you eat, reflect on the food in the plate and be grateful. People often confuse gratefulness with religion, but it is more of a spiritual endeavour. Practising gratitude before a meal gives us the opportunity to realise the efforts of the soil, the farmer, the sun, the water, and the universe invested in delivering you your meal from farm to fork.

Prefacing your food with gratitude honours the meal and helps you be conscious of consumption and wastage.

GRATITUDE: THE ART AND PRACTICE OF EVERYDAY STILLNESS

Practising gratitude can help you eat mindfully and experience the calmness we are stripped of in today's busy life.

1. Visualise the journey of food

Pause and imagine the fields and farmlands that produced the food on your plate. Think of all the efforts, care, and love devoted to raising the vegetables, fruits, and meat placed before you.

2. Pause to experience the aroma

Eating engages all your senses, while we only tend to focus on the sense of taste. Scientists explain that focusing on the aroma of the food releases chemicals in the body that aid digestion. Engage your sense of smell and show gratitude for the ability to experience various aromas.

3. Make an affirmation

Make a personal gratitude affirmation that relates to you and allows you to immerse yourself in an experience of genuine appreciation for the food on your plate. Prepare your mind for consumption and believe that it will nourish your mind, body and soul.

The purpose of affirmations is twofold. One is to show gratitude for the food on your plate, and the second is to redirect the pattern of your mind towards a more balanced relationship with food.

As previously discussed, the mind and gut are interlinked. Positive affirmations are simple statements that help you reframe behaviour and feelings that directly influence the health of your gut.

CHAPTER 10

A WINNING MENU

COOKING PASSION AND CREATIVITY

Food is one of our basic needs and takes centre stage in all events in our life. Food is not only a source of nourishment, comfort, and relief, but is a vital ingredient of our social interactions. Food is sacred, and preparing it with your mind and soul is insightful and awakening. The process of cooking teaches us to be mindful and embrace creativity.

As humans, we are accustomed to activities that help us practice our creative instincts. These activities mostly involve tasks in which we have to create things physically. We realise our creative physical work that engages our mind, body, and soul, leaving physical proof. Painting, gardening, writing, crafts, and cooking are different types of activities through which we experience the joy of creativity. Oftentimes, we don't even realise how creative work brings us satisfaction and becomes an outlet for peace and joy.

Collecting ingredients, chopping, slicing, mincing, mixing, and rolling them on the counter: every step involved in the process of cooking is full of opportunities to practice consciousness and creativity. A pinch of this, a spoon of that—constantly engaging the eye and the mind to ensure all ingredients are in place. Peeking, smelling, and tasting the meal through parts is as exciting as it is awakening.

COOKING ENHANCES MINDFULNESS

The daily grind of life in this fast-paced world keeps us distracted from time for ourselves. Mindful living is not a practice based on science; it is a continual process of self-analysis. Cooking is a journey towards self-awareness.

Anyone familiar with the Zen master Dogen and his writing would know that the cook holds the highest position in the monastery. The instructions for Tenzo by Zenji Dogen claim that a cook has a "way-seeking mind" and is responsible for the wellbeing of other monks in the monastery. Zen masters refer to a fulfilled life as a "supreme meal," one that is prepared through consciousness, spirituality, knowledge, and hard work.

When master Dogen inquired of his cook why he did not engage any helpers when drying the mushrooms in the sun, he responded, "I am not like other people," meaning there is no purpose in cooking if you are not doing it yourself.

In embracing this kind of mindfulness through ordinary acts such as cooking, even the simplest of ingredients reveal their true self to us. As Dogen says, "Handle even a single leaf of green in such a way that it manifests the body of the Buddha.

Cooking is an excellent way to awaken senses and practice mindfulness. In a mindful state, a person is open to the present and aware of the sensual experiences. And while mindfulness requires practice, cooking is a ritualistic approach that helps enhance your ability to be more aware of everything.

Engaging both mind and body, cooking allows us to put all our senses at work, attentively and intentionally engaging them in the process of preparing food. From slicing the vegetables to washing rice, concentrating deeply helps our mind communicate to our hands and our hands communicate to our mind.

With mindfulness, we can connect and relate to the task we have accomplished. If we consciously analyse our ingredients, mix and match flavours, then the way we prepare the meal and eat it can contribute to a heightened experience of mindfulness.

Just as yoga triggers emotions and helps us develop an awareness of our body, mindful cooking also enables us to approach different sensations with care and curiosity. The popping of the corn, the aroma of basil, and the texture of soft peas are all here to serve a purpose. The play of sounds, texture, taste, and smell involves our senses and our whole body in the experience of cooking.

Many people who follow a vegetarian diet benefit from the nourishing properties of a plant-based diet. Mindful cooking is also a conscious approach towards conscious eating that helps us understand the benefits and side effects of the food we put on our plates.

Compare chopping carrots to practising mastery of knife skills required to julienne the same carrot. What seems like a minor task to some is mastery for others. Practising new techniques and cooking skills allows us to explore our capacity to experiment with different things. It opens a field of passion and creativity that shows us a way into our inner narrative.

Are you scared of the feedback? Do you tend to avoid making mistakes? Do you run from recipes that are hard to make? Do you feel satisfied by positive feedback?

These are all little messages that reveal to you the different sides of your own personality.

HEALTH AND WELLNESS ON A PLATE

From consciousness comes the awareness and realisation of what to eat and what not to eat. By practising consciousness and regulating the flows of mind and body, we tend to make healthier choices that are beneficial for our health. So, what do consciously aware people add to their plates?

1. Fruits and vegetables. Aim for variety and colour in your plate through fresh and organic vegetables and fruits.

2. Opt for whole grains. According to the Healthy Eating Plate, whole grains must make up to half of your plate. Intact whole grains, including oats, barley, whole wheat, and brown rice, are healthier than refined grains, as they keep a check and balance on the body's insulin and blood sugar levels.

3. Plant-based oils. Consuming plant-based oils in moderation, instead of hydrogenated oils, help us prevent the consumption of trans fat, which increases cholesterol levels and disturbs the lipid profile of the liver. Plant-based oils include sunflower, soy, canola, olive, and peanut oil, among many others.

4. Power from protein. Protein must take up a quarter of the plate. Nuts, beans, poultry, and fish are healthy sources of protein that are easy to consume and fast to digest. Avoid processed foods such as sausages and bacon with little to no nutritional level.

5. Hydrate. Drink eight glasses of fresh, clean water daily, and limit the intake of sugary, processed drinks.

A healthy diet tends to focus on the quality of the food. The type of carbohydrates we consume is more important than how many carbohydrates we consume in a meal. The best and most beneficial sources of carbohydrates are fruits, vegetables, beans, and whole grains, the essentials of a good diet.

Sugary beverages have the highest calorie count with little to no benefit for the body. Consuming a higher than required amount of sugar only puts a burden on the gut.

Contrary to popular belief, a healthy diet must include healthy sources of fat. A low-fat diet is highly recommended to sustain and maintain energy in the body.

GOOD HEALTH ON A BUDGET

Achieving health on a budget is not about hunting low-cost foods on sale items, but avoiding impulse purchases when hungry or enticed by food marketing. Food waste is a leading cause of money loss, as people allow healthy food items to spoil without distributing or preparing them.

Shopping consciously and preventing food wastage are the two significant behavioural changes of the many others that help you achieve good health on a budget. Consider the following when heading to your next grocery trip:

1. Plan your meals. Shopping carelessly results from a lost mind. If you want to eat healthy without wasting money, plan your meals, so your shopping list includes only those ingredients.

2. Opt for meatless options. Health authorities state that the ideal meat consumption per week is three portions. Alternatively, a plant-based diet is a better source of protein and is highly nutritious. Compared to meat, plant-based meals are more budget-friendly. But if you crave meat, you can prepare recipes that include 70% of plant-based proteins and only 30% of meat. This saves you money and increases the heartiness of the meal.

3. Purchase filling snacks. Snacking is one of our favourite eating habits. Any diet plan that pushes us to avoid snacking risks failure, as most of us do not have access to full-time meals during work. Although we can't skip snacks, we can choose what to eat. For example, a handful of nuts are more fulfilling than a pack of chips. Chowing down an apple will give you more energy than a can of Coke. Unsatiating foods such as chips, soda, and biscuits make people want to consume more. Replace unsatiating foods with satiating and healthy snacks such as fruits, nuts, granola bars, etc.

4. Make a flexible shopping list. Avoid purchasing perishable food items in extra quantities for later use. Buy fresh fruits and vegetables rather than frozen ones. Maintain flexibility in your list to opt for items with a higher utility for you in the kitchen.

5. Buy staple foods in bulk. The upfront cost of buying food in bulk may seem higher than usual, but it's the cost per unit is less. Buy family-size packs of dry beans, whole grains, and lentils.

6. Eat attentively. There are many benefits of mindfulness, and one of the most important ones is that it automatically controls our portion of the meal. Practising mindfulness while eating can lead to feeling satisfied with a small portion.

7. Skip processed food. As humans, we are tempted by convenience. Convenience in the kitchen with ready-made foods has cost us our health and money. While it is tempting and easy to prepare, making the same meals at home is usually a cheaper and healthier option.

8. Buy local. The produce at a farmers' market is fresher than grocery stores, as they only pluck when the fruit is ripened. By contrast, grocery stores pick fruits and vegetable before ripening, to ensure they last longer during distribution. Local produce is mostly more nutritious, healthier, and cost-friendly.

SEAFOOD AND ITS BENEFITS FOR GOOD HEALTH AND LONGEVITY

Whether you want to prevent heart attack, depression, or dementia, eating a small portion of seafood regularly can help. The Dietary Guidelines for America recently published a diet that is gut-friendly, nutrient-dense, and helpful in fighting against various diseases. Research proves that eating seafood reduces the risk of a range of health problems.

Consuming seafood regularly is most beneficial for the heart. The omega-3 content found in seafood plays a vital role in helping maintain a healthy heart rate, lowering blood pressure, preventing cardiac disturbances, and improving vessel function.

Eating seafood every week minimises the risk of ischemic stroke, heart disease, and heart failure. Seafood has benefits not only for the heart but also the liver, skin, and immunity. People who suffer from high cholesterol levels can opt for a diet based on seafood and plants, which will lower triglycerides, maintain lipid profile, and prevent liver failure.

Other health benefits of consuming fish and seafood include:

- ❖ People who consume good fish are 20% less likely to have anxiety and depression. The fatty acids in the fish are an effective treatment for gastrointestinal disorders and associated depression.
- ❖ People who consume seafood have a 14% larger hippocampus. People with a larger hippocampus generally have a lower chance of being diagnosed with Alzheimer's.
- ❖ Adults with a higher level of omega-3s in the body are likely to live longer.
- ❖ Seafood is an excellent source of fatty acids, omega-3s and energy for pregnant women. Research shows that babies have 5.8 points higher IQ levels if their mother consumed seafood.

However, certain types of seafood do more harm than good. Pollutants make their way into our everyday diet, and seafood is no exception. Certain types of seafood can be contaminated with mercury, pesticide residue, and polychlorinated biphenyls. Mercury can damage the nervous system and cause nerve damages.

Avoid eating swordfish, Pangasius, golden snapper, shark, or king mackerel, as they have the highest levels of mercury. Choose local catch and less unique forms of fish.

DISHING UP WINNING RECIPES

1. ONE-POT KALE AND QUINOA PILAF

Ingredients:

- 1 cup rinsed quinoa
- 2 cups salted water
- 1 lemon juiced and zested
- A bunch kale, rinsed and chopped
- 1 tablespoon walnut oil
- 2 minced scallions
- 3 tablespoons pine nuts
- ¼ cup feta or goat cheese

Preparation:

In a covered pot, bring water to a boiling point and add quinoa. Lower the heat and cover the pot. Let the quinoa simmer for 8-10 minutes. Once soft, add kale and cover again. Let the quinoa and kale simmer for 5 minutes. Turn the heat off, and let the kale cook on steam for another 5 minutes.

Take a large bowl and combine scallions, lemon juice, pine nuts, walnut oil, and goat cheese. When ready, kale will be bright green and quinoa firm but tender.

Mix quinoa and kale mixture with the remaining ingredients. Toss and season with salt and pepper. One-Pot Kale and Quinoa pilaf is ready to be served.

2. ABSURDLY ADDICTIVE ASPARAGUS

Ingredients:

1 tablespoon butter

4 ounces diced pancetta

1 pound trimmed and sliced asparagus

2 cloves minced and chopped garlic

¼ cup thinly sliced leek

1 teaspoon orange zest

A handful pine nuts

Chopped Italian parsley as per need

Ground pepper and salt for seasoning

Preparation:

Sauté diced pancetta in a non-stick pan over medium heat. Keep stirring until the pancetta is lightly golden and crisp.

Now add butter to the pan and put leek and asparagus in melted butter. Toss and stir till the asparagus is tender-crisp. The ideal cooking time for asparagus should be less than 4 minutes.

Now add garlic, orange, and lemon zest. Sprinkle parsley, pine nuts, salt, and pepper. Sauté for another 1 minute. Serve immediately.

###

3. LENTIL AND MINCED BEEF SOUP FOR COLD WINTER NIGHTS

Ingredients:

1 lb ground beef

2 teaspoon olive oil

½ cup chopped onion

1 tablespoon dried parsley

1 tablespoon crushed, chopped garlic

1 teaspoon dry parsley

½ cup celery finely chopped

1 teaspoon ground cumin

2 cups chicken broth

4 cups beef broth

2 cups water

½ cup thinly sliced carrots

2 cups lentils

½ cup brown rice

2 tablespoons vinegar

Preparation:

In a heated pan, add olive oil and ground beef. Cook until brown. Set aside, and add celery and onion to the same pan with additional olive oil, if required. Cook until the onions are translucent and celery is soft.

Now add garlic, cumin, parsley, and thyme and sauté for a few minutes.

Add the cooked beef and vegetables to the soup pot. Add chicken broth, beef broth, and 2 cups of water to the pot. Also, add chopped carrots, and allow the soup to cook.

Once it reaches the boiling point, add lentils and simmer for another 60 minutes. When the lentils become tender, add rice and cook for another 20-30 minutes or until the rice are ready. Add more water if required.

Now season the soup with salt, pepper, and vinegar. Serve hot.

###

4. Eggplant and courgette parmesan Bake

Ingredients:

700g sliced aubergines.

1 tablespoon olive oil

1 finely chopped onion

2 sliced courgettes in half-centimetre strips

1 finely chopped red pepper

2-3 cloves crushed garlic

1 chopped tomato

1 teaspoon dry oregano

120g low-fat mozzarella

50g finely grated Parmesan cheese

Preparation:

Preheat the oven to 180 degrees. Set courgettes and aubergines in the tray and grill from both sides until light brown. Now add olive oil to the pan and toss in the onion. Cook until translucent over medium heat.

Add red pepper and mix the combination for 5 minutes. Now combine tomatoes, garlic, and oregano, and simmer on low heat for 5 minutes. Your sauce is ready.

In an ovenproof dish, add sauce, and top with courgette and aubergine slices. Add another layer of sauce, and spread parmesan cheese. Add another layer of aubergine and courgette, and repeat until all slices are combined. On the top layer, add the remaining sauce, mozzarella, and parmesan cheese.

Bake for 30 minutes or until golden brown. Sprinkle salt and pepper and serve.

5. CINNAMON SUGAR BREAKFAST PUFFS

Ingredients:

1/3 cup unsalted butter

½ cup white sugar

1 egg

½ cup all-purpose flour

¼ teaspoon nutmeg

½ teaspoon baking powder

¼ teaspoon allspice

½ teaspoon salt

Pinch ginger powder

Pinch clove powder

1 teaspoon orange zest

½ cup whole milk, room temperature

Cinnamon-sugar coating

½ cup granulated sugar

1 teaspoon powdered cinnamon

6 tablespoons melted butter

Preparation:

In a heavy pan, heat butter over medium heat. Keep stirring to prevent the butter from burning, and cook until brown with a nutty smell. Pour the batter into a mixing bowl. Let the butter cool and come to room temperature.

Preheat the oven to 350F.

In a bowl, add egg, sugar, and butter. Beat until combined and fluffy. The ideal time for beating with an electric mixer is 5 minutes.

In a separate bowl, combine baking powder, flour, spices, zest, and salt in a separate bowl. Add all dry ingredients to the butter mixture and mix well. Slowly add butter mix until fluffy.

Grease the muffin cups with oil, and evenly add batter to the cups. Bake for 20 minutes or until fragrant and golden brown.

For the coating, combine sugar and cinnamon powder. In a separate bowl, add melted butter. Once the muffins are ready, dip in butter and then the sugar-cinnamon mixture. Puffs are now ready to be served.

CONCLUSION

There is a strong relationship between our brain and our gut. And because of this connection, our emotions, such as sadness, depression, anxiety, fear, and anger, affect the health of our gut and vice versa. Research has proven that our gut and brain are not two systems, but are linked through millions of nerves responsible for the constant communication between our mind and gut.

Gut microbiota hosts trillions of microorganisms in our intestines and are responsible for promoting health and maintaining a healthy nervous system. Conversely, disturbances in gut microbiota can contribute to depression, fatigue, and various other diseases. Maintaining a healthy gut microbiota is only possible through lifestyle change. Research proves that food and mindfulness are two sources of health that eliminate any need for medication.

Opting for a minimally processed, plant-based, and higher-fibre diet can increase gut microbiota and regulate brain activity.

Science recognises the positive effects of mindful eating, smaller portions, and a fresh diet. By giving purposeful attention to our food, mindful eating is a method that focuses on sensual awareness of the experience of food. Mindful eating makes us more aware of what we consume and changes our association with food by encouraging a more health-driven holistic perspective to eat.

There are various methods of practising mindfulness, and cooking is one of the most promising one. It is an excellent way to awaken senses and give insight into self. In a mindful state, a person is open to the present and aware of the sensual experiences. And while mindfulness requires practice, cooking is a ritualistic approach that helps enhance your ability to be more aware of everything.

Gut health, eating mindfully, and cooking are all parts of the same boat when a person journeys towards holistic wellbeing.

ACKNOWLEDGEMENTS

I would like to thank and acknowledge Mr. Geoffrey Semaganda of Action Wealth Publishing. Also, the two great professors whom I met during my university journey, Dr. Martin Kessler (University of Bonn Germany) and Dr. Neil Macdonald (University of Roehampton South West London).

ABOUT THE AUTHOR

Dorine Mwesigwa was born in Uganda to Mr. Geddy Mwesigwa and Mrs. Margaret Mwesigwa. In her twenties, she relocated to the United Kingdom, which is where she spent most of her motherhood years, before relocating to Germany, where she spent five years. After that, she returned to and settled in the United Kingdom.

Dorine is also the author of *Iron Eagle Mum,* a book that describes her trials, tribulations, and experiences in the three countries where she has lived: Uganda, the United Kingdom, and Germany. In that book, Dorine shares a message of resilience and hope. No matter what happens to you in life, you can overcome it, learn from it, and use it as ammunition to become a stronger, better, and wiser person, plus make a difference in other people's lives with the example you set.

From her adversities, she set out on a journey of passion: passion for food, cooking, healthy nutrition, and scientific research on plant-based and other kinds of diets and nutrition.

Printed in Great Britain
by Amazon